ULYSSES S. GRANT
1822 1885

Chronology - Documents - Bibliographical Aids

Edited by
PHILIP R. MORAN

Series Editor
HOWARD F. BREMER

Oceana Publications, Inc.
Dobbs Ferry, New York 10522
1968

Library of Congress Catalog Card Number 68-23568
Oceana Book No. 303-6

PRINTED IN THE UNITED STATES OF AMERICA

CONTENTS 88890

BIBLIOGRAPHICAL AIDS

NAME INDEX

EDITOR'S FOREWORD

Every attempt has been made to cite the most accurate dates in this Chronology. Diaries, documents, and similar evidence have been used to determine the exact date. If, however, later scholarship has found such dates to be obviously erroneous, the more plausible date has been used. Should this Chronology be in conflict with other authorities, the student is urged to go back to original sources as well as to such competent scholars as Bruce Catton and Allan Nevins.

This is a research tool compiled primarily for the student. While it does make some judgments on the significance of the events, it is hoped that they are reasoned judgments based on a long acquaintance with American History.

Obviously, the very selection of events by any writer is itself a judgment.

The essence of these little books is in their making available some pertinent facts and key documents **plus** a critical bibliography which should direct the student to investigate for himself additional and/or contradictory material. The works cited may not always be available in small libraries, but neither are they usually the old, out of print type of books often included in similar accounts. Documents in this volume are taken from: James D. Richardson, ed., **Messages and Papers of the Presidents.** Vol. VII; **Washington.** 1897.

CHRONOLOGY

CHRONOLOGY

YOUTH AND EARLY ARMY SERVICE

1822

April 27 Born: Point Pleasant, Ohio, as Hiram Ulysses Grant. Father: Jesse; Mother: Hannah Simpson.

1823

Family moved to Georgetown, Ohio. In his youth, "Lyss" helped his father on farm and in tannery, developed horsemanship. Studied in Georgetown and in academies at Maysville, Kentucky (1836-37), and Ripley, Ohio (1838-39).

1839

July 1 Entered United States Military Academy at West Point. Listed by Congressman Thomas L. Hamer as Ulysses Simpson, Grant adopted the change and gained nickname Uncle Sam, or Sam. A mediocre scholar, he liked mathematics. Was the best horseman at the academy.

1843

June Graduated from West Point 21st in a class of 39. Commissioned brevet second lieutenant, 4th U.S. Infantry Regiment.

September 30 Joined regiment at Jefferson Barracks near St. Louis. Remained there until the following spring, when the regiment moved to Louisiana.

1845

September Promoted to full second lieutenant. Sailed with regiment from New Orleans to Corpus Christi to join General Zachary Taylor.

1846

May 8 Fought in his first battle, Palo Alto, near the Rio Grande, at start of the Mexican War. Fought the next day at Resaca de la Palma. He was appointed that summer as regimental quartermaster and commissary.

1

September 23   Braved enemy fire in volunteer horse ride during battle of Monterey.

1847

March 29   Vera Cruz capitulated after siege. Grant served with General Winfield Scott in this and all subsequent battles in campaign to take Mexico City.

September 8   Breveted first lieutenant for gallant conduct in battle of Molino del Rey.

September 13   Breveted captain for gallant conduct in battle of Chapultepec. Outside Mexico City's San Cosme gate, he set up howitzer in church belfry to bombard enemy.

September 16   Commissioned first lieutenant. Fighting ceased and Grant remained in Mexico until the following July. As commissary, he bought flour, hired Mexicans to bake bread for the troops, and, he later wrote, "I made more money for the (regimental) fund than my pay amounted to during the whole war."

1848

August 22   Married Julia Boggs Dent, sister of a West Point classmate, in St. Louis. She outlived him. Until the spring of 1852, he was stationed at Sackets Harbor, New York, and in Detroit area.

1850

May 30   Son, Frederick Dent, born in St. Louis.

1852

July 5   Sailed for Isthmus of Panama on way to Pacific Coast duty. Arrived at Fort Vancouver in Oregon Territory in September. His wife remained at his father's home in Bethel, Ohio.

July 22   Second son, Ulysses Simpson Jr., born in Bethel.

1853

August 5   Commissioned captain. Headed company at Humboldt Bay, California, under Brevet Colonel Robert C. Buchanan. Grant's drinking, which developed during this period, led to friction between the two officers.

1854

April 11   Resigned from Army after drinking incident. Resignation became effective July 31. Until 1858, Grant unsuccessfully farmed land outside St. Louis given to him by his father-in-law. He occasionally sold cordwood in the city.

1855

July 4   Daughter, Ellen (Nellie) Wrenshall, born in Wish-ton-wish, Missouri.

1858

February 6 Third son, Jesse Root, born in St. Louis.

1859

January 1   Entered unsuccessful real estate agency partnership with Henry Boggs.

1860

May   Started as clerk in father's leather store in Galena, Illinois.

CIVIL WAR

1861

April 15   Lincoln called for volunteers after attack on Fort Sumter. Grant helped drill the Galena company and accompanied it to Springfield. There he worked in the adjutant general's office and was mustering officer.

June 17   Commissioned colonel of the 21st Illinois Volunteer Infantry by Governor Richard Yates.

August 7   Appointed brigadier general of volunteers by Lincoln. His commission was dated May 17.

September 4 Established headquarters in Cairo, Illinois, in command of district of southern Illinois and southeastern Missouri. Appointed by Major General John C. Fremont.

September 6 Occupied Paducah, Kentucky, to keep it out of Confederate hands.

November 7 Attacked Confederate camp at Belmont, Missouri.

November 9 Fremont succeeded by Major General Henry W. Halleck.

1862

February 6 Captured Fort Henry on the Tennessee River in joint attack with gunboats of Commodore A.H. Foote.

February 16 Captured Fort Donelson, Tennessee, in first major Northern victory of war. Derived nickname, "Unconditional

Surrender" Grant, from terms he gave to Confederate Brigadier General Simon Bolivar Buckner. The latter gave up with 14,000 men. Depicted as leading troops with an unlit cigar in his mouth, Grant subsequently received over 10,000 cigars from admirers.

February 16   Named major general of volunteers.

April 6   Unintrenched Union troops under Grant were attacked and driven back by Confederates under General Albert S. Johnston at Shiloh (Pittsburg Landing), Tennessee. Next day, reinforced Union soldiers drove off the enemy. Casualties totaled 24,000, of which 13,000 were Union losses. When Grant was abused as allegedly drunk and negligent at Shiloh, Lincoln replied, "I can't spare this man. He fights."

October 25   Named commander of Department of the Tennessee.

November 2   Began Vicksburg campaign.

1863

January 1   Lincoln issued Emancipation Proclamation.

May 19 and 22   Attacked heavily fortified Vicksburg.

July 4   Accepted surrender of General John C. Pemberton and 30,000 troops after six-week siege of Vicksburg. Promoted to major general in the U. S. Army.

October 16   Named general of Union armies in the West.

Nov. 23-25   Routed Southern troops under General Braxton Bragg at Lookout Mountain and Missionary Ridge, thus gaining control of Chattanooga, major east-west railroad junction.

1864

March 9   Received commission as lieutenant general, U.S. Army, from Lincoln at Executive Mansion. Put in command of all Union armies three days later.

May 5   Began six-week campaign with the Army of the Potomac. Battles included the Wilderness (May 5-6), Spotsylvania Court House (May 8-12) and Cold Harbor (June 1-3). Union casualties totaled 55,000 and Grant was called "butcher." At Spotsylvania, he wrote: "I propose to fight it out on this line if it takes all summer."

June 8   Lincoln renominated by Republicans for Presidency by 484 votes to Grant's 22 on first ballot.

June 15-18   Attacked Petersburg in unsuccessful attempt to cut off Richmond from the remainder of the South. A nine-month siege begun.

1865

April 2   Lee evacuated Petersburg and Richmond. Grant pursued him toward Lynchburg.

April 9   Accepted Lee's surrender of 28,000 men at Appomattox Court House.

April 14   Declined invitation to join President and Mrs. Lincoln at Ford's Theatre performance so that he and Mrs. Grant might visit their children at school in Burlington, New Jersey. Lincoln killed.

May 23-24   With President Johnson, witnessed grand review of Union armies in Washington, D.C.

INTERLUDE

1866

July 25   Commissioned four-star General of the Army by Congress.

1867

March 2   Command of the Army Act became law. It required that the President issue all military orders through the General of the Army (Grant). This act figured in later unsuccessful impeachment of Johnson.

August 12   Appointed Secretary of War, ad interim, by Johnson, who had suspended Edwin M. Stanton.

1868

January 13   Resigned as Secretary when Congress returned Stanton to the post. The President then accused Grant of bad faith in resigning.

May 20-21   Nominated Republican candidate for the Presidency on first ballot at convention in Chicago. His running mate was Schuyler Colfax of Indiana. Grant's brief acceptance speech concluded, "Let us have peace," a motto later carved on his tomb.

November 3 Elected president by a popular majority of 306,000 out of 5,700,000 votes over Horatio Seymour, Democrat, of Indiana. Grant captured 26 of 34 states and 214 of 294 electoral votes.

FIRST TERM

1869

March 4 Sworn in as 18th President by Chief Justice Salmon P. Chase at the Capitol. The brief inaugural address stressed payment of the war debt and a return to specie basis.

March 5 Cabinet members named: Secretary of State Elihu B. Washburne of Illinois; Attorney General Ebenezer R. Hoar of Massachusetts; Postmaster General John A.J. Creswell of Maryland; Secretary of the Navy Adolph E. Borie of Pennsylvania; Secretary of the Interior Jacob D. Cox of Ohio.

Grant consulted no Republican leaders in making the Cabinet appointments. Even some of the appointees had not known they would be named. Alexander T. Stewart, New York merchant, was unable to accept the Treasury post because of an old law forbidding appointment of a businessman as Secretary.

March 11 Hamilton Fish of New York named to replace Washburne (he began duties on March 17). Secretary of the Treasury George S. Boutwell of Massachusetts and Secretary of War John A. Rawlins of Illinois took up duties.

March 18 Signed Public Credit Act, which provided that Government obligations were to be paid in gold.

April 12 Nomination of John Lothrop Motley as Minister to England announced.

May 10 Union Pacific and Central Pacific railroads joined at Promontory, Utah.

May 14 Designated July 6 for Virginians to vote on a new constitution.

June 4   Cabinet approved Secretary Fish's plan for the United States to mediate between Spain and Cuba to secure the latter's independence. The revolt had started the previous October. The mediation attempt failed.

June 15   Entertained by Jay Gould and James Fisk on steamboat trip to Boston. The financiers, seeking to corner the gold market, sought to influence Grant not to sell Government gold. The President's brother-in-law, Abel R. Corbin, was involved in the scheme.

June 25   Replaced Borie as Secretary of the Navy by George M. Robeson of New Jersey.

July 13   Proclaimed November 30 as day for vote on new Mississippi constitution.

July 15   Designated November 30 for Texans to ratify or reject their new constitution.

July 17   Orville E. Babcock, Grant's personal secretary, sailed for Santo Domingo to get data about the country. Annexation of Santo Domingo was a major aim of Grant. Buenaventura Baez was president at the time.

August 5   Visited Hamilton Fish at Garrison, New York. The President spent much of the summer touring the East.

September 6 Rawlins died.

September 11 William T. Sherman of Ohio became Secretary of War.

September 14 Babcock arrived back in Washington from Santo Domingo. He had signed treaty of annexation while there, although he had no diplomatic authority.

September 24 Financial panic followed "Black Friday" drop in gold price. To foil Gould-Fisk scheme, Grant had ordered the Treasury to sell gold. However, some of taint remained on Grant.

November 1 William W. Belknap of Iowa succeeded Sherman as Secretary of War.

November 29 Babcock, back in Santo Domingo, and Dominicans signed treaty of annexation prepared by Fish. Congressional approval required.

December 6 First annual message called for early action to stabilize currency.

December 24 Stanton, former Secretary of War, died.

1870

January 10 Submitted treaty of annexation of Santo Domingo to the Senate.

February 7 Legal Tender Act declared unconstitutional by Supreme Court in regard to debts contracted before the act was passed. The vote was 4-3 in the case of *Hepburn vs. Griswold.* The same day Grant, who disapproved of the decision, nominated William Strong of Pennsylvania and Joseph P. Bradley of New Jersey to the two vacant Supreme Court posts.

February 18 Strong appointed to Supreme Court.

March 21 Bradley appointed to Supreme Court. Legal Tender issues were then reopened.

March 23 Urged Congress in special message to take steps to revive the nation's merchant marine.

March 30 Fifteenth Amendment declared ratified.

May 31 Signed Ku Klux Klan Act. Supported by Grant, this enforcement act permitted Federal intervention in South to protect rights of Negro voters.

June 13 Sent message to Congress urging against recognition of Cuban rebels as belligerents. Fish feared that such recognition would lead to war between Spain and the United States. The House followed Grant's recommendation.

June 22 Signed bill creating Department of Justice.

June 30 Senate rejected Santo Domingo treaty, a major defeat for Grant. Angered at opposition of Charles Sumner, chairman of the Senate Foreign Relations Committee, Grant had him deposed as chairman the following March 10.

July 1   Asked Fish to nominate a replacement for Motley, an ally of Sumner, as Minister to England. Motley was recalled.

July 8   Amos T. Akerman of Georgia replaced Hoar as Attorney General.

August 22   Declared the United States neutral in Franco-Prussian conflict.

November 1   Columbus Delano of Ohio became Secretary of the Interior.

December 5   Second annual message reviewed Santo Domingo affair and United States relations with Spain and England, and called for civil service reform.

1871

February 9   Named United States commissioners to serve on a Joint High Commission with English representatives. Major concern was the dispute over damages done to Union shipping during Civil War by *Alabama* and other Confederate raiders built in Great Britain.

February 27 Commission began deliberations.

March 3   Signed Civil Service Act.

March 4   Appointed George W. Curtis first chairman of the Civil Service Commission. Congress did not support reforms. Curtis resigned in 1875.

April 20   Signed second Ku Klux Klan Bill designed to enforce Fourteenth Amendment.

May 1   In *Knox vs. Lee* decision, the Supreme Court declared the Legal Tender Acts constitutional, by a 5-4 vote, reversing the *Hepburn* decision. Grant was accused of packing the court by his appointment of Strong and Bradley.

May 8   Treaty of Washington signed with Great Britain, ending quarrels over "*Alabama* claims," North Atlantic fishing rights, use of Canadian-American waterways and the Northwest boundary. The treaty provided that an international tribunal would decide on the questions.

October 8 Chicago fire killed over 250 persons, destroyed more than 17,000 buildings.

October 12 Issued proclamation calling upon violators of the Fourteenth Amendment in nine South Carolina counties to disperse. Five days later he suspended habeus corpus there. Under martial law, more than 7,000 persons were indicted under the enforcement act of April 20.

December 4 In third annual message, Grant called for a law that would enforce caution on those persons recommending others for public positions.

December 15 Geneva Tribunal set up under Treaty of Washington began deliberations.

1872

January 1 Put Civil Service Act into effect.

January 10 George H. Williams of Oregon became Attorney General, succeeding Akerman.

April 19 Reported to House on activities of the Klan in South Carolina, where its members used violence and murder to keep Negroes from voting.

May 14 Sent special message to Congress urging legislation to protect immigrants on shipboard and after arrival.

May 22 Signed Amnesty Act restoring civil rights to all Southerners except certain former Confederate leaders.

June 5-6 Nominated on first ballot for a second term by Republicans meeting in Philadelphia. His running mate was Henry Wilson of Massachusetts. They were opposed by Democratic and Liberal Republican nominees Horace Greeley of New York and Benjamin G. Brown of Missouri. There were also "Straight-out Democrat" and Prohibition Party candidates. "Turn the rascals out" was the Greeley campaign cry. He criticized Grant's administration as corrupt and vengeful toward the South.

August 25 Under the Treaty of Washington, the Geneva Tribunal awarded the United States $15,000,000 for the "*Alabama* claims."

September 4   Credit Mobilier scandal broke. Grant associates, including the vice president, vice president nominee and several Congressmen, were accused of accepting stock in the Union Pacific's camouflage company in return for favors.

September 14   Geneva Tribunal concluded sessions.

October 21   Northwest boundary decided under Treaty of Washington. The Emperor of Germany was the arbiter.

November 5   Elected to a second term by a 763,000 popular majority. Grant gained 286 out of 352 electoral votes and took 29 of 35 states.

November 29   Greeley died. Electoral votes for him were split among several persons.

December 2   Fourth annual message noted Grant's regret that strife continued in Cuba, the rebellion still unsettled after four years.

December 11   Appointed Ward Hunt of New York to the Supreme Court.

1873

February 12   Signed Coinage Act demonetizing silver and making gold the sole standard. This act was later called "the crime of '73."

February 14   Urged Congress to strengthen Federal district courts in the Utah Territory.

February 27   Representatives Oakes Ames of Massachusetts and James Brooke of New York censured in Credit Mobilier scandal.

March 3   Signed "Salary Grab" Act increasing salaries of Congressmen and other Government officials, and doubling the President's. A loud public outcry followed. Timber Culture Act and Coal Lands Act signed.

SECOND TERM

March 4   Sworn into office for second term, due to be marked by numerous scandals. A snow storm raged during the ceremony. In inaugural address, Grant said he felt his re-election was his vindication after being the subject of "abuse and slander scarcely ever equaled in political history."

His Cabinet remained unchanged (Fish, Boutwell, Belknap, Williams, Creswell, Robeson, Delano).

March 17   William A. Richardson of Massachusetts took office as Secretary of the Treasury.

May 7   Chief Justice Chase died in New York City.

September 18   Failure of Jay Cooke banking firm led to general crash and depression. Much unemployment resulted.

October 31   Spanish captured *Virginius*, flying U.S. flag illegally, running arms to Cuban rebels. Some of crew, including Americans, shot as pirates. Resulting reaction in the United States brought war with Spain close. Skill of Secretary of State Fish helped abate crisis. He later gained indemnity of $80,000 for families of executed Americans.

December 1   Fifth annual message included statement that the experience of the current financial panic had proven that the nation's currency "is the best that has ever been devised."

1874

January 20   "Salary Grab" Act repealed except for salary increases of President and Supreme Court justices.

January 21   Appointed Morrison R. Waite of Ohio as Chief Justice.

April 22   Vetoed Inflation Act, which would have increased paper money in circulation.

May 15   Declared Elisha Baxter the legally elected governor of Arkansas. The state legislature had thrown out the claim of Joseph Brooks.

May 21   Nellie Grant and Englishman Algernon Sartoris wed at White House. After a few years they separated.

June 4   Benjamin H. Bristow of Kentucky became Secretary of the Treasury, succeeding Richardson. The latter had resigned to evade Congressional censure in the Sanborn Contract scandal.

July 7   James W. Marshall of Virginia assumed post of Postmaster General.

September 1   Marshall Jewell of Connecticut succeeded Marshall.

September 15   Issued proclamation backing Louisiana state government of William P. Kellogg, in dispute over validity of his election as governor in 1872.

December 7   Strongly urged establishment of a stable currency, in his sixth annual message.

December 15   Hosted visiting king of Hawaii.

1875

January 13   Sent message to Congress explaining use of Federal troops to expel members of the Louisiana legislature from the State House on January 4 at the request of Governor Kellogg.

January 14   Signed Specie Resumption Act. Advocated by Grant, the act helped stabilize currency by calling for specie payments to resume on January 1, 1879, and for reduction of greenbacks in circulation.

January 30   Commercial reciprocity treaty signed with Hawaii.

February 8   In a message to the Senate, Grant declared that Brooks—not Baxter—was the lawfully elected governor of Arkansas.

March 1   Signed Civil Rights Act designed to protect rights of Negroes in public places and to forbid further denial of their right to serve on juries.

May 10   Whisky Ring exposed in St. Louis. Revenue officials and distillers had been pocketing tax revenues on whisky. Investigation by Secretary of the Treasury Bristow led to 238 indictments. "Let no guilty man escape," said Grant, before it was revealed that Babcock, his secretary, was involved.

May 15   Edwards Pierrepont of New York entered post of Attorney General, succeeding Williams.

May 31   Ruled out third term in letter to newspaper.

July 31   Former President Johnson died.

September 29   Addressed reunion of Army of the Tennessee at Des Moines, Iowa, urging support of education.

October 19   Zachariah Chandler of Michigan replaced Delano as Secretary of the Interior.

November 22   Vice President Henry Wilson died in Washington.

December 7   In his seventh annual message, Grant called for universal education of children, encouragement of literacy by voting restrictions, separation of church and state, elimination of polygamy and enactment of sound currency laws.

December 9   Babcock indicted on Whisky Ring charge.

                                      1876

February 24   Babcock acquitted, largely because of support by Grant.

March 2   House voted to impeach Secretary of War Belknap for taking bribes for sale of trading posts in West. Belknap resigned the same day, although Grant came to his defense.

March 11   Alphonso Taft of Ohio became Secretary of War.

May 4   In reply to the House, Grant asserted the right of the President to perform his official duties away from Washington. No act of Congress can "limit, suspend or confine" this right, he stated.

May 10   International Centennial Exposition opened in Philadelphia.

June 1   Alphonso Taft moved to the Attorney General post and James D. Cameron of Pennsylvania became Secretary of War.

June 5   James G. Blaine read part of "Mulligan letters" before House in attempt to dispel charges of implication in shady railroad transactions. The revelations cost him the Republican nomination for the Presidency.

June 14-16   Republicans meeting in Cincinnati nominated Rutherford B. Hayes of Ohio as Presidential candidate.

June 25   General Custer's troops massacred by Indians at Little Big Horn, Montana.

June 26   Issued centennial proclamation.

June 27-29   Samuel J. Tilden of New York nominated by the Democrats, meeting in St. Louis, to oppose Hayes.

July 4   Country marked 100th year of existence.

July 7   Lot M. Morrill of Maine succeeded Bristow as Secretary of the Treasury.

July 12   James N. Tyner of Indiana became Postmaster General.

August 1   Declared Colorado a state.

               Senate failed to convict Belknap of malfeasance in office. Although few Senators doubted his guilt, those who voted for acquittal felt the Senate had no jurisdiction because Belknap had resigned.

October 17   In proclamation, Grant warned night-riding terrorist "rifle clubs" in South Carolina to disband.

November 7   Tilden gained popular vote margin of 250,000 in election but his victory was disputed.

December 5   Apologized, in final annual message, for mistakes during his administration. "Failures have been errors of judgment, not of intent," Grant told Congress.

1877

January 22   At request of the House, Grant reported on use of Federal troops to suppress violence in portions of the South since the preceding August 1.

January 29   Signed bill establishing an Electoral Commission to decide Hayes-Tilden dispute.

January 31   Commission met. Voting was along party lines for Hayes.

February 9   Transmitted to Congress a memorial from the committee of New York citizens appointed to cooperate in plan for erection of Statue of Liberty. The French presented the statue to the United States in 1884 and it was dedicated two years later.

March 2	Hayes declared President at joint session of Congress.

March 3 | Hayes took private oath as President (March 4 was a Sunday).

Desert Land Act signed. Grant's second term ended.

March 5 | Hayes inaugurated.

RETIREMENT

May 17 | Sailed from Philadelphia on *S. S. Indiana* on 28-month tour of Europe, the Holy Land, Egypt and the Orient.

1879
September 20 | Docked in San Francisco on return to the United States. Grant was welcomed at receptions across the country. His political advisors, aiming for a third-term nomination for him, suggested he absent himself so as not to dissipate the enthusiasm for him. Grant toured Cuba and Mexico that winter.

1880
June 2-5, 7-8 | Lost to James A. Garfield on 36th ballot in bid for the Republican nomination for the Presidency. Grant had led on first ballot with 304 ballots, against seven candidates.

1881
August | Bought mansion in New York City after a stay in Galena. The building was bought through the generosity of friends. A trust fund of $250,000 was also set up for the ex-President.

1883
December 24 | Hurt hip in fall. Grant always used a cane thereafter.

1884
May 4 | Borrowed $150,000 from William H. Vanderbilt to help in crisis involving Grant and Ward investment firm. The firm failed through the duplicity of Ferdinand Ward, who was later sentenced to prison. Grant was left practically penniless.

1885

February 21   Began dictating *Memoirs.*

March 3   Congressional act aided the nearly destitute Grant by authorizing addition of general to list of retired Army officers, with pay.

April 2   Ill with terminal cancer of the throat, Grant was baptized a Methodist by the Rev. J.P. Newman.

July   Completed *Memoirs* a few days before his death. Published by Mark Twain the same year, it brought $500,000 in royalties to Grant's family.

July 23   Died at Mount McGregor, in upstate New York. His body was buried in Riverside Park in New York City, and was interred in Grant's Tomb there on April 27, 1897.

DOCUMENTS

DOCUMENTS

FIRST INAUGURAL ADDRESS
March 4, 1869

Grant sought little advice in preparing this brief address, whose moderate tone on Reconstruction was not borne out by his Administration.

Citizens of the United States:

Your suffrages having elected me to the office of President of the United States, I have, in conformity to the Constitution of our country, taken the oath of office prescribed therein. I have taken this oath without mental reservation and with the determination to do to the best of my ability all that is required of me. The responsibilities of the position I feel, but accept them without fear. The office has come to me unsought; I commence its duties untrammeled. I bring to it a conscious desire and determination to fill it to the best of my ability to the satisfaction of the people.

On all leading questions agitating the public mind I will always express my views to Congress and urge them according to my judgment, and when I think it advisable will exercise the constitutional privilege of interposing a veto to defeat measures which I oppose; but all laws will be faithfully executed, whether they meet my approval or not.

I shall on all subjects have a policy to recommend, but none to enforce against the will of the people. Laws are to govern all alike—those opposed as well as those who favor them. I know no method to secure the repeal of bad or obnoxious laws so effective as their stringent execution.

The country having just emerged from a great rebellion, many questions will come before it for settlement in the next four years which preceding Administrations have never had to deal with. In meeting these it is desirable that they should be approached calmly, without prejudice, hate, or sectional pride, remembering that the greatest good to the greatest number is the object to be attained.

This requires security of person, property, and free religious and political opinion in every part of our common country, without regard to local prejudice. All laws to secure these ends will receive my best efforts for their enforcement.

A great debt has been contracted in securing to us and our posterity the Union. The payment of this, principal and interest, as well as the return to a specie basis as soon as it can be accomplished without material detriment to the debtor class or the country at large, must be provided for. To protect the national honor, every dollar of Government indebtedness should be paid in gold, unless otherwise expressly stipulated in the contract. Let it be understood that no repudiator of one farthing of our public debt will be trusted in public place, and it will go far toward strengthening a credit which ought to be the best in the world, and will ultimately enable us to replace the debt with bonds bearing less interest than we now pay. To this should be added a faithful collection of the revenue, a strict accountability to the Treasury for every dollar collected, and the greatest practicable retrenchment in expenditure in every department of Government.

When we compare the paying capacity of the country now, with the ten States in poverty from the effects of war, but soon to emerge, I trust, into greater prosperity than ever before, with its paying capacity twenty-five years ago, and calculate what it probably will be twenty-five years hence, who can doubt the feasibility of paying every dollar then with more ease than we now pay for useless luxuries? Why, it looks as though Providence had bestowed upon us a strong box in the precious metals locked up in the sterile mountains of the far West, and which we are now forging the key to unlock, to meet the very contingency that is now upon us.

Ultimately it may be necessary to insure the facilities to reach these riches, and it may be necessary also that the General Government should give its aid to secure this access; but that should only be when a dollar of obligation to pay secures precisely the same sort of dollar to use now, and not before. Whilst the question of specie payments is in abeyance the prudent business man is careful about contracting debts payable in the distant future. The nation should follow the same rule. A prostrate commerce is to be rebuilt and all industries encouraged.

The young men of the country—those who from their age must be its rulers twenty-five years hence—have a peculiar interest in maintaining the national honor. A moment's reflection as to what will be our commanding influence among the nations of the earth in their day, if they are only true to themselves, should inspire them with national pride. All divisions—geographical, political, and religious—can join in this common sentiment. How the public debt is to be paid or specie payments resumed is not so important as that a plan should be adopted and acquiesced in. A united determination to do is worth more than divided counsels upon the method of doing. Legislation upon this subject may not be necessary now, nor even advisable, but it will be when the civil law is more fully restored in all parts of the country and trade resumes its wonted channels.

It will be my endeavor to execute all laws in good faith, to collect all revenues assessed, and to have them properly accounted for and economically disbursed. I will to the best of my ability appoint to office those only who will carry out this design.

In regard to foreign policy, I would deal with nations as equitable law requires individuals to deal with each other, and I would protect the law-abiding citizen, whether of native or foreign birth, wherever his rights are jeopardized or the flag of our country floats. I would respect the rights of all nations, demanding equal respect for our own. If others depart from this rule in their dealings with us, we may be compelled to follow their precedent.

The proper treatment of the original occupants of this land—the Indians—is one deserving of careful study. I will favor any course toward them which tends to their civilization and ultimate citizenship.

The question of suffrage is one which is likely to agitate the public so long as a portion of the citizens of the nation are excluded from its privileges in any State. It seems to me very desirable that this question should be settled now, and I entertain the hope and express the desire that it may be by the ratification of the fifteenth article of amendment to the Constitution.

In conclusion I ask patient forbearance one toward another throughout the land, and a determined effort on the part of every citizen to do his share toward cementing a happy union; and I ask the prayers of the nation to Almighty God in behalf of this consummation.

ON VIRGINIA'S CONSTITUTION
April 7, 1869

In the continuing efforts to restore legal governments to all of the 11 former Confederate states, Congress on April 10 authorized designation of dates for voting on new constitutions for Virginia, Mississippi and Texas.

To the Senate and House of Representatives:

While I am aware that the time in which Congress proposes now to remain in session is very brief, and that it is its desire, as far as is consistent with the public interest, to avoid entering upon the general business of legislation, there is one subject which concerns so deeply the welfare of the country that I deem it my duty to bring it before you.

I have no doubt that you will concur with me in the opinion that it is desirable to restore the States which were engaged in the rebellion to their proper relations to the Government and the country at as early a period as the people of those States shall be found willing to become peaceful and orderly communities and to adopt and maintain such constitutions and laws as will effectually secure the civil and political rights of all persons within their borders. The authority of the United States, which has been vindicated and established by its military power, must undoubtedly be asserted for the absolute protection of all its citizens in the full enjoyment of the freedom and security which is the object of a republican government; but whenever the people of a rebellious State are ready to enter in good faith upon the accomplishment of this object, in entire conformity with the constitutional authority of Congress, it is certainly desirable that all causes of irritation should be removed as promptly as possible, that a more perfect union may be established and the country be restored to peace and prosperity.

The convention of the people of Virginia which met in Richmond on Tuesday, December 3, 1867, framed a constitution for that State, which was adopted by the convention on the 17th of April, 1868, and I desire respectfully to call the attention of Congress to the propriety of providing by law for the holding of an election in that State at some time during the months of May and June next, under the direction of the military commander of that district, at which the question of the adoption of that constitution shall be submitted to the citizens of the State; and if this should seem desirable, I would recommend that a separate vote be taken upon such parts as may be thought expedient, and that at the same time and under the same authority there shall be an election for the officers provided under such constitution, and that the constitution, or such parts thereof as shall have been adopted by the people, be submitted to Congress on the first Monday of December next for its consideration, so that if the same is then approved the necessary steps will have been taken for the restoration of the State of Virginia to its proper relations to the Union. I am led to make this recommendation from the confident hope and belief that the people of that State are now ready to cooperate with the National Government in bringing it again into such relations to the Union as it ought as soon as possible to establish and maintain, and to give to all its people those equal rights under the law which were asserted in the Declaration of Independence in the words of one of the most illustrious of its sons.

I desire also to ask the consideration of Congress to the question whether there is not just ground for believing that the constitution framed by a convention of the people of Mississippi for that State, and once rejected, might not be again submitted to the people of that State in like manner, and with the probability of the same result.

ON INDIAN AFFAIRS
June 3, 1869

Westward expansion increased conflict with Indians. Grant believed the answer was to place the Indians on reservations under Federal supervision.

Washington, D. C., June 3, 1869

A commission of citizens having been appointed under the authority of law to cooperate with the administrative departments in the management of Indian affairs, consisting of William Welsh, of Philadelphia; John V. Farwell, of Chicago; George H. Stuart, of Philadelphia; Robert Campbell, St. Louis; W. E. Dodge, New York; E. S. Tobey, Boston; Felix R. Brunot, Pittsburgh; Nathan Bishop, New York, and Henry S. Lane, of Indiana, the following regulations will till further directions control the action of said commission and of the Bureau of Indian Affairs in matters coming under their joint supervision:

1. The commission will make its own organization and employ its own clerical assistants, keeping its "necessary expenses of transportation, subsistence, and clerk hire when actually engaged in said service" within the amount appropriated therefor by Congress.

2. The commission shall be furnished with full opportunity to inspect the records of the Indian Office and to obtain full information as to the conduct of all parts of the affairs thereof.

3. They shall have full power to inspect, in person or by subcommittee, the various Indian superintendencies and agencies in the Indian country, to be present at payment of annuities, at consultations or councils with the Indians, and when on the ground to advise superintendents and agents in the performance of their duties.

4. They are authorized to be present, in person or by subcommittee, at purchases of goods for Indian purposes, and inspect said purchases, advising the Commissioner of Indian Affairs in regard thereto.

5. Whenever they shall deem it necessary or advisable that instructions of superintendents or agents be changed or modified, they will communicate such advice through the office of Commissioner of Indian Affairs to the Secretary of the Interior, and in like manner their advice as to changes in modes of purchasing foods or conducting the affairs of the Indian Bureau proper. Complaints against superintendents or agents or other officers will in the same manner be forwarded to the Indian Bureau or Department of the Interior for action.

6. The commission will at their board meetings determine upon the recommendations to be made as to the plans of civilizing or dealing with the Indians, and submit the same for action in the manner above indicated, and all plans involving the expenditure of public money will be acted upon by the Executive or the Secretary of the Interior before expenditure is made under the same.

7. The usual modes of accounting with the Treasury can not be changed, and all expenditures, therefore, must be subject to the approvals now required by law and the regulations of the Treasury Department, and all vouchers must conform to the same laws and requirements and pass through the ordinary channels.

8. All the officers of the Government connected with the Indian service are enjoined to afford every facility and opportunity to said commission and their subcommittees in the performance of their duties, and to give the most respectful heed to their advice within the limits of such officers' positive instructions from their superiors; to allow such commissioners

full access to their records and accounts, and to cooperate with them in the most earnest manner to the extent of their proper powers in the general work of civilizing the Indians, protecting them in their legal rights, and stimulating them to become industrious citizens in permanent homes, instead of following a roving and savage life.

9. The commission will keep such records or minutes of their proceedings as may be necessary to afford evidence of their action, and will provide for the manner in which their communications with and advice to the Government shall be made and authenticated.

A PROCLAMATION
October 5, 1869

This Thanksgivings Day proclamation reflects the lessening of the tensions of war and its aftermath.

The year which is drawing to a close has been free from pestilence; health has prevailed throughout the land; abundant crops reward the labors of the husbandman; commerce and manufactures have successfully prosecuted their peaceful paths; the mines and forests have yielded liberally; the nation has increased in wealth and in strength; peace has prevailed, and its blessings have advanced every interest of the people in every part of the Union; harmony and fraternal intercourse restored are obliterating the marks of past conflict and estrangement; burdens have been lightened; means have been increased; civil and religious liberty are secured to every inhabitant of the land, whose soil is trod by none but freemen.

It becomes a people thus favored to make acknowledgment to the Supreme Author from whom such blessings flow of their gratitude and their dependence, to render praise and thanksgiving for the same, and devoutly to implore a continuance of God's mercies.

Therefore I, Ulysses S. Grant, President of the United States, do recommend that Thursday, the 18th day of November next, be observed as a day of thanksgiving and of praise and of prayer to Almighty God, the creator and the ruler of the all the people of the United States to accustomed places of public worship and to unite in the homage and praise due to the bountiful Father of All Mercies and in fervent prayer for the continuance of the manifold blessings he has vouchsafed to us as a people.

In testimony whereof I have hereunto set my hand and caused the seal of the United States to be affixed, this 5th day of October, A.D. (SEAL) 1869, and of the Independence of the United States of America the ninety-fourth.

U. S. GRANT

By the President:
HAMILTON FISH, *Secretary of State*

FIRST ANNUAL MESSAGE
December 6, 1869

*Grant's suggestion that Congress give "due consider-
ation" to raising the salaries of Government officials
preshadowed the ill-received "Salary Grab" Act of
1873. Important features of this message were his call
for a return to specie payments and his reactions to
the Cuba conflict.*

To the Senate and House of Representatives:

In coming before you for the first time as Chief Magistrate of this
great nation, it is with gratitude to the Giver of All Good for the many
benefits we enjoy. We are blessed with peace at home, and are without
entangling alliances abroad to forebode trouble; with a territory unsur-
passed in fertility, of an area equal to the abundant support of 500,000,000
people, and abounding in every variety of useful mineral in quantity
sufficient to supply the world for generations; with exuberant crops. . . .
Happily, harmony is being rapidly restored within our own borders. . . .

Emerging from a rebellion of gigantic magnitude, aided, as it was, by
the sympathies and assistance of nations with which we were at peace,
eleven States of the Union were, four years ago, left without legal State
governments. . . .

Seven States which passed ordinances of secession have been fully
restored to their places in the Union. The eighth (Georgia) held an election at which she ratified her constitution, republican in form, elected a
governor, Members of Congress, a State legislature, and all other officers
required. The governor was duly installed, and the legislature met and
performed all the acts then required of them by the reconstruction acts
of Congress. Subsequently, however, in violation of the constitution
which they had just ratified (as since decided by the supreme court of the
State), they unseated the colored members of the legislature and admitted
to seats some members who are disqualified by the third clause of the
fourteenth amendment to the Constitution—an article which they themselves had contributed to ratify. Under these circumstances I would submit to you whether it would not be wise, without delay, to enact a law
authorizing the governor of Georgia to convene the members originally
elected to the legislature, requiring each member to take the oath prescribed by the reconstruction acts, and none to be admitted who are
ineligible under the third clause of the fourteenth amendment.

The freedmen, under the protection which they have received, are
making rapid progress in learning, and no complaints are heard of lack
of industry on their part where they receive fair remuneration for their
labor. . . .

Among the evils growing out of the rebellion, and not yet referred to, is that of an irredeemable currency. . . . I earnestly recommend to you, then, such legislation as will insure a gradual return to specie payments and put an immediate stop to fluctuations in the value of currency.

The methods to secure the former of these results are as numerous as are the speculators on political economy. To secure the latter I see but one way, and that is to authorize the Treasury to redeem its own paper, at a fixed price, whenever presented, and to withhold from circulation all currency so redeemed until sold again for gold. . . .

As the United States is the freest of all nations, so, too, its people sympathize with all people struggling for liberty and self-government; but while so sympathizing it is due to our honor that we should abstain from enforcing our views upon unwilling nations and from taking an interested part, *without invitation,* in the quarrels between different nations or between governments and their subjects. . . . For more than a year a valuable province of Spain, and a near neighbor of ours, in whom all our people can not but feel a deep interest, has been struggling for independence and freedom. The people and Government of the United States entertain the same warm feelings and sympathies for the people of Cuba in their pending struggle that they manifested throughout the previous struggles between Spain and her former colonies in behalf of the latter. But the contest has at no time assumed the conditions which amount to a war in the sense of international law, or which would show the existence of a *de facto* political organization of the insurgents sufficient to justify a recognition of belligerency. . . .

The United States, in order to put a stop to bloodshed in Cuba, and in the interest of a neighboring people, proposed their good offices to bring the existing contest to a termination. The offer, not being accepted by Spain on a basis which we believed could be received by Cuba, was withdrawn. . . .

The subject of an interoceanic canal to connect the Atlantic and Pacific oceans through the Isthmus of Darien is one in which commerce is greatly interested. Instructions have been given to our minister to the Republic of the United States of Columbia to endeavor to obtain authority for a survey by this Government, in order to determine the practicability of such an undertaking, and a charter for the right of way to build, by private enterprise, such a work, if the survey proves it to be practicable. . . .

Toward the close of the last Administration a convention was signed at London for the settlement of all outstanding claims between Great Britain and the United States, which failed to receive the advice and consent of the Senate to its ratification. . . .

Believing that a convention thus misconceived in its scope and inadequate in its provisions would not have produced the hearty, cordial settlement of pending questions, which alone is consistent with the relations which I desire to have firmly established between the United States and Great Britain, I regarded the action of the Senate in rejecting the treaty to have been wisely taken in the interest of peace and as a necessary step in the direction of a perfect and cordial friendship between the two countries. . . . I hope that the time may soon arrive when the two Governments can approach the solution of this momentous question with an appreciation of what is due to the rights, dignity, and honor of each, and with the determination not only to remove the causes of complaint in the past, but to lay the foundation of a broad principle of public law which will prevent future differences and tend to firm and continued peace and friendship.

This is now the only grave question which the United States has with any foreign nation. . . .

Our manufactures are increasing with wonderful rapidity under the encouragement which they now receive. . . .

On my assuming the responsible duties of Chief Magistrate of the United States it was with the conviction that three things were essential to its peace, prosperity, and fullest development. First among these is strict integrity in fulfilling all our obligations; second, to secure protection to the person and property of the citizen of the United States in each and every portion of our common country, wherever he may choose to move, without reference to original nationality, religion, color, or politics, demanding of him only obedience to the laws and proper respect for the rights of others; third, union of all the States, with equal rights, indestructible by any constitutional means.

To secure the first of these, Congress has taken two essential steps: First, in declaring by joint resolution that the public debt shall be paid, principal and interest, in coin; and second, by providing the means for paying. Providing the means, however, could not secure the object desired without a proper administration of the laws for the collection of the revenues and an economical disbursement of them. To this subject the Administration has most earnestly addressed itself, with results, I hope, satisfactory to the country. . . .

It may be well to mention here the embarrassment possible to arise from leaving on the statute books the so-called "tenure-of-office acts," and to earnestly recommend their total repeal. It could not have been the intention of the framers of the Constitution, when providing that appointments made by the President should receive the consent of the Senate, that the latter should have the power to retain in office persons placed there by Federal appointment against the will of the President. . . .

For the second requisite to our growth and prosperity time and a firm but humane administration of existing laws (amended from time to time as they may prove ineffective or prove harsh and unnecessary) are probably all that are required.

The third can not be attained by special legislation, but must be regarded as fixed by the Constitution itself and gradually acquiesced in by force of public opinion.

From the foundation of the Government to the present the management of the original inhabitants of this continent—the Indians—has been a subject of embarrassment and expense, and has been attended with continuous robberies, murders, and wars. From my own experience upon the frontiers and in Indian countries, I do not hold either legislation or the conduct of the whites who come most in contact with the Indian blameless for these hostilities. The past, however, can not be undone, and the question must be met as we now find it. I have attempted a new policy toward these wards of the nation (they can not be regarded in any other light than as wards), with fair results so far as tried, and which I hope will be attended ultimately with great success. . . .

The building of railroads, and the access thereby given to all the agricultural and mineral regions of the country, is rapidly bringing civilized settlements into contact with all the tribes of Indians. No matter what ought to be the relations between such settlements and the aborigines, the fact is they do not harmonize well, and one or the other has to give way in the end. A system which looks to the extinction of a race is too horrible for a nation to adopt without entailing upon itself the wrath of all Christendom and engendering in the citizen a disregard for human life and the rights of others, dangerous to society. I see no substitute for such a system, except in placing all the Indians on large reservations, as rapidly as it can be done, and giving them absolute protection there. . . .

The report of the Secretary of the Interior shows that the quantity of public lands disposed of during the year ending the 30th of June, 1869, was 7,666,152 acres, exceeding that of the preceding year by 1,010,409 acres. Of this amount, 2,899,544 acres were sold for cash and 2,737,365 acres entered under the homestead laws. . . .

During the last fiscal year 23,196 names were added to the pension rolls and 4,876 dropped therefrom, leaving at its close 187,963. The amount paid to pensioners, including the compensation of disbursing agents, was $28,422,884, an increase of $4,411,902 on that of the previous year. . . .

During the year ending the 30th of September, 1869, the Patent Office issued 13,762 patents, and its receipts were $686,389, being $213,926 more than the expenditures. . . .

I desire respectfully to call the attention of Congress to the inadequate salaries of a number of the most important offices of the Government. In this message I will not enumerate them, but will specify only the justices of the Supreme Court. No change has been made in their salaries for fifteen years. Within that time the labors of the court have largely increased and the expenses of living have at least doubled. During the same time Congress has twice found it necessary to increase largely the compensation of its own members, and the duty which it owes to another department of the Government deserves, and will undoubtedly receive, its due consideration.

There are many subjects not alluded to in this message which might with propriety be introduced, but I abstain, believing that your patriotism and statesmanship will suggest the topics and the legislation most conducive to the interests of the whole people. On my part I promise a rigid adherence to the laws and their strict enforcement.

ON THE MERCHANT MARINE
March 23, 1870

To aid in building up the nation's economy, Grant advocated legislative support of the shipping industry.

EXECUTIVE MANSION
Washington, D. C., March 23, 1870

To the Senate and House of Representatives:

In the Executive message of December 6, 1869, to Congress the importance of taking steps to revive our drooping merchant marine was urged, and a special message promised at a future day during the present session, recommending more specifically plans to accomplish this result. Now that the committee of the House of Representatives intrusted with the labor of ascertaining "the cause of the decline of American commerce" has completed its work and submitted its report to the legislative branch of the Government, I deem this a fitting time to execute that promise.

The very able, calm, and exhaustive report of the committee points out the grave wrongs which have produced the decline in our commerce. It is a national humiliation that we are now compelled to pay from twenty to thirty million dollars annually (exclusive of passage money, which we should share with vessels of other nations) to foreigners for doing the work which should be done by American vessels, American built, American owned, and American manned. This is a direct drain upon the resources of the country of just so much money, equal to casting it into the sea, so far as this nation is concerned.

A nation of the vast and ever-increasing interior resources of the United States, extending, as it does, from one to the other of the great oceans of the world, with an industrious, intelligent, energetic population, must one day possess its full share of the commerce of these oceans, no matter what the cost. Delay will only increase this cost and enhance the difficulty of attaining the result.

I therefore put in an earnest plea for early action in this matter, in a way to secure the desired increase of American commerce. The advanced period of the year and the fact that no contracts for shipbuilding will probably be entered into until this question is settled by Congress, and the further fact that if there should be much delay all large vessels contracted for this year will fail of completion before winter sets in, and will therefore be carried over for another year, induces me to request your early consideration of this subject.

I regard it of such grave importance, affecting every interest of the country to so great an extent, that any method which will gain the end will secure a rich national blessing. Building ships and navigating them utilizes vast capital at home; it employs thousands of workmen in their construction and manning; it creates a home market for the products of the farm and the shop; it diminishes the balance of trade against us precisely to the extent of freights and passage money paid to American vessels, and gives us a supremacy upon the seas of inestimable value in case of foreign war.

Our Navy at the commencement of the late war consisted of less than 100 vessels, of about 150,000 tons and a force of about 8,000 men. We drew from the merchant marine, which had cost the Government nothing, but which had been a source of national wealth, 600 vessels, exceeding 1,000,000 tons, and about 70,000 men, to aid in the suppression of the rebellion.

This statement demonstrates the value of the merchant marine as a means of national defense in time of need.

The Committee on the Causes of the Reduction of American Tonnage, after tracing the causes of its decline, submit two bills, which, if adopted, they believe will restore to the nation its maritime power. Their report shows with great minuteness the actual and comparative American tonnage at the time of its great prosperity; the actual and comparative decline since, together with the causes; and exhibits all other statistics of material interest in reference to the subject. As the report is before Congress, I will not recapitulate any of its statistics, but refer only to the methods recommended by the committee to give back to us our lost commerce.

As a general rule, when it can be adopted, I believe a direct money subsidy is less liable to abuse than an indirect aid given to the same enterprise. In this case, however, my opinion is that subsidies, while they may be given to specified lines of steamers or other vessels, should not be exclusively adopted, but, in addition to subsidizing very desirable lines of ocean traffic, a general assistance should be given in an effective way. I therefore commend to your favorable consideration the two bills proposed by the committee and referred to in this message.

ON THE FIFTEENTH AMENDMENT
March 30, 1870

President Grant broke precedent to express his thoughts on enfranchisement of the Negro.

EXECUTIVE MANSION, March 30, 1870

To the Senate and House of Representatives:

It is unusual to notify the two Houses of Congress by message of the promulgation, by proclamation of the Secretary of State, of the ratification of a constitutional amendment. In view, however, of the vast importance of the fifteenth amendment to the Constitution, this day declared a part of that revered instrument, I deem a departure from the usual custom justifiable. A measure which makes at once 4,000,000 people voters who were heretofore declared by the highest tribunal in the land not citizens of the United States, nor eligible to become so (with the assertion that "at the time of the Declaration of Independence the opinion was fixed and universal in the civilized portion of the white race, regarded as an axiom in morals as well as in politics, that black men had no rights which the white man was bound to respect"), is indeed a measure of grander importance than any other one act of the kind from the foundation of our free Government to the present day.

Institutions like ours, in which all power is derived directly from the people, must depend mainly upon their intelligence, patriotism, and industry. I call the attention, therefore, of the newly enfranchised race to the importance of their striving in every honorable manner to make themselves worthy of their new privilege. To the race more favored heretofore by our laws I would say, Withhold no legal privilege of advancement to the new citizen. The framers of our Constitution firmly believed that a republican government could not endure without intelligence and education generally diffused among the people. The Father of his Country, in his Farewell Address, uses this language:

Promote, then, as an object of primary importance, institutions for the general diffusion of knowledge. In proportion as the structure of a government gives force to public opinion, it is essential that public opinion should be enlightened.

In his first annual message to Congress the same views are forcibly presented, and are again urged in his eighth message.

I repeat that the adoption of the fifteenth amendment to the Constitution completes the greatest civil change and constitutes the most important event that has occurred since the nation came into life. The change will be beneficial in proportion to the heed that is given to the urgent recommendations of Washington. If these recommendations were important then, with a population of but a few millions, how much more important now, with a population of 40,000,000, and increasing in a rapid ratio. I would therefore call upon Congress to take all the means within their constitutional powers to promote and encourage popular education throughout the country, and upon the people everywhere to see to it that all who possess and exercise political rights shall have the opportunity to acquire the knowledge which will make their share in the Government a blessing and not a danger. By such means only can the benefits contemplated by this amendment to the Constitution be secured.

ON THE DOMINICAN REPUBLIC
May 31, 1870

This almost impassioned plea for annexation of the Caribbean republic went unheeded by the Senate.

EXECUTIVE MANSION, May 31, 1870

To the Senate of the United States:

I transmit to the Senate, for consideration with a view to its ratification, an additional article to the treaty of the 29th of November last, for the annexation of the Dominican Republic to the United States, stipulating for an extension of time for exchanging the ratifications thereof, signed in this city on the 14th instant by the plenipotentiaries of the parties.

It was my intention to have also negotiated with the plenipotentiary of San Domingo amendments to the treaty of annexation to obviate objections which may be urged against the treaty as it is now worded; but on reflection I deem it better to submit to the Senate the propriety of their amending the treaty as follows: First, to specify that the obligations of this Government shall not exceed the $1,500,000 stipulated in the treaty; secondly, to determine the manner of appointing the agents to receive and disburse the same; thirdly, to determine the class of creditors who shall take precedence in the settlement of their claims; and, finally, to insert such amendments as may suggest themselves to the minds of Senators to carry out in good faith the conditions of the treaty submitted to the Senate of the United States in January last, according to the spirit and intent of that treaty. From the most reliable information I can obtain, the sum specified in the treaty will pay every just claim against the Republic of San Domingo and leave a balance sufficient to carry on a Territorial government until such time as new laws for providing a Territorial revenue can be enacted and put in force.

I feel an unusual anxiety for the ratification of this treaty, because I believe it will redound greatly to the glory of the two countries interested, to civilization, and to the extirpation of the institution of slavery.

The doctrine promulgated by President Monroe has been adhered to by all political parties, and I now deem it proper to assert the equally important principle that hereafter no territory on this continent shall be regarded as subject of transfer to a European power.

The Government of San Domingo has voluntarily sought this annexation. It is a weak power, numbering probably less than 120,000 souls, and yet possessing one of the richest territories under the sun, capable of supporting a population of 10,000,000 people in luxury. The people of San Domingo are not capable of maintaining themselves in their present condition, and must look for outside support.

They yearn for the protection of our free institutions and laws, our progress and civilization. Shall we refuse them?

I have information which I believe reliable that a European power stands ready now to offer $2,000,000 for the possession of Samana Bay alone. If refused by us, with what grace can we prevent a foreign power from attempting to secure the prize?

The acquisition of San Domingo is desirable because of its geographical position. It commands the entrance to the Caribbean Sea and the Isthmus transit of commerce. It possesses the richest soil, best and most capacious harbors, most salubrious climate, and the most valuable products of the forests, mine, and soil of any of the West India Islands. Its possession by us will in a few years build up a coastwise commerce of immense magnitude, which will go far toward restoring to us our lost merchant marine. It will give to us those articles which we consume so largely and do not produce, thus equalizing our exports and imports.

In case of foreign war it will give us command of all the islands referred to, and thus prevent an enemy from ever again possessing himself of rendezvous upon our very coast.

At present our coast trade between the States bordering on the Atlantic and those bordering on the Gulf of Mexico is cut into by the Bahamas and the Antilles. Twice we must, as it were, pass through foreign countries to get by sea from Georgia to the west coast of Florida.

San Domingo, with a stable government, under which her immense resources can be developed, will give remunerative wages to tens of thousands of laborers not now on the island.

This labor will take advantage of every available means of transportation to abandon the adjacent islands and seek the blessings of freedom and its sequence—each inhabitant receiving the reward of his own labor. Porto Rico and Cuba will have to abolish slavery, as a measure of self-preservation to retain their laborers.

San Domingo will become a large consumer of the products of Northern farms and manufactories. The cheap rate at which her citizens can be furnished with food, tools, and machinery will make it necessary that the contiguous islands should have the same advantages in order to compete in the production of sugar, coffee, tobacco, tropical fruits, etc. This will open to us a still wider market for our products.

The production of our own supply of these articles will cut off more than one hundred millions of our annual imports, besides largely increasing our exports. With such a picture it is easy to see how our large debt abroad is ultimately to be extinguished. With a balance of trade against us (including interest on bonds held by foreigners and money spent by our citizens traveling in foreign lands) equal to the entire yield of the precious metals in this country, it is not so easy to see how this result is to be otherwise accomplished.

The acquisition of San Domingo is an adherence to the "Monroe Doctrine;" it is a measure of national protection; it is asserting our just claim to a controlling influence over the great commercial traffic soon to flow from east to west by the way of the Isthmus of Darien; it is to build up our merchant marine; it is to furnish new markets for the products of our farms, shops, and manufactories; it is to make slavery insupportable in Cuba and Porto Rico at once and ultimately so in Brazil; it is to settle the unhappy condition of Cuba, and end an exterminating conflict; it is to provide honest means of paying our honest debts, without overtaxing the people; it is to furnish our citizens with the necessaries of everyday life at cheaper rates than ever before; and it is, in fine, a rapid stride toward that greatness which the intelligence, industry, and enterprise of the citizens of the United States entitle this country to assume among nations.

ON THE CUBAN REBELLION
June 13, 1870

The Cuban rebellion against Spain, which was to extend for a decade, raised delicate diplomatic problems for the United States, where sympathy was largely with the rebels.

To the Senate and House of Representatives:

In my annual message to Congress at the beginning of its present session I referred to the contest which had then for more than a year existed in the island of Cuba between a portion of its inhabitants and the Government of Spain, and the feelings and sympathies of the people and Government of the United States for the people of Cuba, as for all peoples struggling for liberty and self-government, and said that "the contest has at no time assumed the conditions which amount to war in the sense of international law, or which would show the existence of a *de facto* political organization of the insurgents sufficient to justify a recognition of belligerency."

During the six months which have passed since the date of that message the condition of the insurgents has not improved, and the insurrection itself, although not subdued, exhibits no signs of advance, but seems to be confined to an irregular system of hostilities, carried on by small and illy armed bands of men, roaming without concentration through the woods and the sparsely populated regions of the island, attacking from ambush convoys and small bands of troops, burning plantations and the estates of those not sympathizing with their cause.

But if the insurrection has not gained ground, it is equally true that Spain has not suppressed it. Climate, disease, and the occasional bullet have worked destruction among the soldiers of Spain; and although the Spanish authorities have possession of every seaport and every town on the island, they have not been able to subdue the hostile feeling which has driven a considerable number of the native inhabitants of the island to armed resistance against Spain, and still leads them to endure the dangers and the privations of a roaming life of guerrilla warfare.

On either side the contest has been conducted, and is still carried on, with a lamentable disregard of human life and of the rules and practices which modern civilization has prescribed in mitigation of the necessary horrors of war. The torch of Spaniard and of Cuban is alike busy in carrying devastation over fertile regions; murderous and revengeful decrees are issued and executed by both parties. Count Valmaseda and Colonel Boet, on the part of Spain, have each startled humanity and aroused the indignation of the civilized world by the execution, each, of a score of prisoners at a time, while General Quesada, the Cuban chief, coolly and with apparent unconsciousness of aught else than a proper act, has admitted the slaughter, by his own deliberate order, in one day, of upward of 650 prisoners of war.

A summary trial, with few, if any, escapes from conviction, followed by immediate execution, is the fate of those arrested on either side on suspicion of infidelity to the cause of the party making the arrest.

Whatever may be the sympathies of the people or of the Government of the United States for the cause or objects for which a part of the people of Cuba are understood to have put themselves in armed resistance to the Government of Spain, there can be no just sympathy in a conflict carried on by both parties alike in such barbarous violation of the rules of civilized nations and with such continued outrage upon the plainest principles of humanity.

We can not discriminate in our censure of their mode of conducting their contest between the Spaniards and the Cubans. Each commit the same atrocities and outrages alike the established rules of war.

The properties of many of our citizens have been destroyed or embargoed, the lives of several have been sacrificed, and the liberty of others has been restrained. In every case that has come to the knowledge of the Government an early and earnest demand for reparation and indemnity has been made, and most emphatic remonstrance has been presented against the manner in which the strife is conducted and against the reckless disregard of human life, the wanton destruction of material wealth, and the cruel disregard of the established rules of civilized warfare.

I have, since the beginning of the present session of Congress, communicated to the House of Representatives, upon their request, an account of the steps which I had taken in the hope of bringing this sad conflict to an end and of securing to the people of Cuba the blessings and the right of independent self-government. The efforts thus made failed, but not without an assurance from Spain that the good offices of this Government might still avail for the objects to which they had been addressed.

During the whole contest the remarkable exhibition has been made of large numbers of Cubans escaping from the island and avoiding the risks of war; congregating in this country, at a safe distance from the scene of danger, and endeavoring to make war from our shores, to urge our people into the fight which they avoid, and to embroil this Government in complications and possible hostilities with Spain. It can scarce be doubted that this last result is the real object of these parties, although carefully covered under the deceptive and apparently plausible demand for a mere recognition of belligerency.

It is stated on what I have reason to regard as good authority that Cuban bonds have been prepared to a large amount, whose payment is made dependent upon the recognition by the United States of either Cuban belligerency or independence. The object of making their value thus contingent upon the action of this Government is a subject for serious reflection.

In determining the course to be adopted on the demand thus made for a recognition of belligerency the liberal and peaceful principles adopted by the Father of his Country and the eminent statesmen of his day, and followed by succeeding Chief Magistrates and the men of their day, may furnish a safe guide to those of us now charged with the direction and control of the public safety.

From 1789 to 1815 the dominant thought of our statesmen was to keep the United States out of the wars which were devastating Europe. The discussion of measures of neutrality begins with the State papers of Mr. Jefferson when Secretary of State. He shows that they are measures of national right as well as of national duty; that misguided individual citizens can not be tolerated in making war according to their own caprice, passions, interests, or foreign sympathies; that the agents of foreign governments, recognized or unrecognized, can not be permitted to abuse our hospitality by usurping the functions of enlisting or equipping military or naval forces within our territory. Washington inaugurated the policy of neutrality and of absolute abstinence from all foreign entangling alliances, which resulted, in 1794, in the first municipal enactment for the observance of neutrality.

The duty of opposition to filibustering has been admitted by every President. Washington encountered the efforts of Genet and of the French revolutionists; John Adams, the projects of Miranda; Jefferson, the schemes of Aaron Burr. Madison and subsequent Presidents had to deal with the question of foreign enlistment or equipment in the United States, and since the days of John Quincy Adams it has been one of the constant cares of Government in the United States to prevent piratical expeditions against the feeble Spanish American Republics from leaving our shores. In no country are men wanting for any enterprise that holds out promise of adventure or of gain.

In the early days of our national existence the whole continent of America (outside of the limits of the United States) and all its islands were in colonial dependence upon European powers.

The revolutions which from 1810 spread almost simultaneously through all the Spanish American continental colonies resulted in the establishment of new States, like ourselves, of European origin, and interested in excluding European politics and the questions of dynasty and of balances of power from further influence in the New World.

The American policy of neutrality, important before, became doubly so from the fact that it became applicable to the new Republics as well as to the mother country.

It then devolved upon us to determine the great international question at what time and under what circumstances to recognize a new power as entitled to a place among the family of nations, as well as the preliminary question of the attitude to be observed by this Government toward the insurrectionary party pending the contest.

Mr. Monroe concisely expressed the rule which has controlled the action of this Government with reference to revolting colonies pending their struggle by saying:

As soon as the movement assumed such a steady and consistent form as to make the success of the Provinces probable, the rights to which they were entitled by the laws of nations as equal parties to a civil war were extended to them.

The strict adherence to this rule of public policy has been one of the highest honors of American statesmanship, and has secured to this Government the confidence of the feeble powers on this continent, which induces them to rely upon its friendship and absence of designs of conquest and to look to the United States for example and moral protection. It has given to this Government a position of prominence and of influence which it should not abdicate, but which imposes upon it the most delicate duties of right and of honor regarding American questions, whether those questions affect emancipated colonies or colonies still subject to European dominion.

The question of belligerency is one of fact, not to be decided by sympathies for or prejudices against either party. The relations between the parent state and the insurgents must amount in fact to war in the sense of international law. Fighting, though fierce and protracted, does not alone constitute war. There must be military forces acting in accordance with the rules and customs of war, flags of truce, cartels, exchange of prisoners, etc.; and to justify a recognition of belligerency there must be, above all, a *de facto* political organization of the insurgents sufficient in character and resources to constitute it, if left to itself, a state among nations capable of discharging the duties of a state and of meeting the just responsibilities it may incur as such toward other powers in the discharge of its national duties.

Applying the best information which I have been enabled to gather, whether from official or unofficial sources, including the very exaggerated statements which each party gives to all that may prejudice the opposite or give credit to its own side of the question, I am unable to see in the present condition of the contest in Cuba those elements which are requisite to constitute war in the sense of international law.

The insurgents hold no town or city; have no established seat of government; they have no prize courts; no organization for the receiving and collecting of revenue; no seaport to which a prize may be carried or through which access can be had by a foreign power to the limited interior territory and mountain fastnesses which they occupy. The existence of a legislature representing any popular constituency is more than doubtful.

In the uncertainty that hangs around the entire insurrection there is no palpable evidence of an election, of any delegated authority, or of any government outside the limits of the camps occupied from day to day by roving companies of insurgent troops; there is no commerce, no trade, either internal or foreign, no manufactures.

The late commander in chief of the insurgents, having recently come to the United States, publicly declared that "all commercial intercourse or trade with the exterior world has been utterly cut off;" and he further added: "To-day we have not 10,000 arms in Cuba."

It is a well-established principle of public law that a recognition by a foreign state of belligerent rights to insurgents under circumstances such as now exist in Cuba, if not justified by necessity, is a gratuitous demonstration of moral support to the rebellion. Such necessity may yet hereafter arrive, but it has not yet arrived, nor is its probability clearly to be seen.

If it be war between Spain and Cuba, and be so recognized, it is our duty to provide for the consequences which may ensue in the embarrassment to our commerce and the interference with our revenue.

If belligerency be recognized, the commercial marine of the United States becomes liable to search and to seizure by the commissioned cruisers of both parties; they become subject to the adjudication of prize courts.

Our large coastwise trade between the Atlantic and the Gulf States and between both and the Isthmus of Panama and the States of South America (engaging the larger part of our commercial marine) passes of necessity almost in sight of the island of Cuba. Under the treaty with Spain of 1795, as well as by the law of nations, our vessels will be liable to visit on the high seas. In case of belligerency the carrying of contraband, which now is lawful, becomes liable to the risks of seizure and condemnation. The parent Government becomes relieved from responsibility for acts done in the insurgent territory, and acquires the right to exercise against neutral commerce all the powers of a party to a maritime war. To what consequences the exercise of those powers may lead is a question which I desire to commend to the serious consideration of Congress.

In view of the gravity of this question, I have deemed it my duty to invite the attention of the war-making power of the country to all the relations and bearings of the question in connection with the declaration of neutrality and granting of belligerent rights.

There is not a *de facto* government in the island of Cuba sufficient to execute law and maintain just relations with other nations. Spain has not been able to suppress the opposition to Spanish rule on the island, nor to award speedy justice to other nations, or citizens of other nations, when their rights have been invaded.

There are serious complications growing out of the seizure of American vessels upon the high seas, executing American citizens without proper trial, and confiscating or embargoing the property of American citizens. Solemn protests have been made against every infraction of the rights either of individual citizens of the United States or the rights of our flag upon the high seas, and all proper steps have been taken and are being pressed for the proper reparation of every indignity complained of.

The question of belligerency, however, which is to be decided upon definite principles and according to ascertained facts, is entirely different from and unconnected with the other questions of the manner in which the strife is carried on on both sides and the treatment of our citizens entitled to our protection.

The questions concern our own dignity and responsibility, and they have been made, as I have said, the subjects of repeated communications with Spain and of protests and demands for redress on our part. It is hoped that these will not be disregarded, but should they be these questions will be made the subject of a further communication to Congress.

A PROCLAMATION
August 22, 1870

This declaration of neutrality in the Franco-Prussian War was followed in October by another proclamation setting forth the conditions under which warships of the belligerents would be permitted to use United States ports.

Whereas a state of war unhappily exists between France on the one side and the North German Confederation and its allies on the other side; and

Whereas the United States are on terms of friendship and amity with all the contending powers and with the persons inhabiting their several dominions; and

Whereas great numbers of the citizens of the United States reside within the territories or dominions of each of the said belligerents and carry on commerce, trade, or other business or pursuits therein, protected by the faith of treaties; and

Whereas great numbers of the subjects or citizens of each of the said belligerents reside within the territory or jurisdiction of the United States and carry on commerce, trade, or other business or pursuits therein; and

Whereas the laws of the United States, without interfering with the free expression of opinion and sympathy, or with the open manufacture or sale of arms or munitions of war, nevertheless impose upon all persons who may be within their territory and jurisdiction the duty of an impartial neutrality during the existence of the contest:

Now, therefore, I, Ulysses S. Grant, President of the United States, in order to preserve the neutrality of the United States and of their citizens and of persons within their territory and jurisdiction, and to enforce their laws, and in order that all persons, being warned of the general tenor of the laws and treaties of the United States in this behalf and of the law of nations, may thus be prevented from an unintentional violation of the same, do hereby declare and proclaim that by the act passed on the 20th day of April, A.D. 1818, commonly known as the "neutrality law," the following acts are forbidden to be done, under severe penalties, within the territory and jurisdiction of the United States, to wit:

1. Accepting and exercising a commission to serve either of the said belligerents, by land or by sea, against the other belligerent.

2. Enlisting or entering into the service of either of the said belligerents as a soldier or as a marine or seaman on board of any vessel of war, letter of marque, or privateer.

3. Hiring or retaining another person to enlist or enter himself in the service of either of the said belligerents as a soldier or as a marine or seaman on board of any vessel of war, letter of marque, or privateer.

4. Hiring another person to go beyond the limits or jurisdiction of the United States with intent to be enlisted as aforesaid.

5. Hiring another person to go beyond the limits of the United States with intent to be entered into service as aforesaid.

6. Retaining another person to go beyond the limits of the United States with intent to be enlisted as aforesaid.

7. Retaining another person to go beyond the limits of the United States with intent to be entered into service as aforesaid. (But the said act is not to be construed to extend to a citizen or subject of either belligerent who, being transiently within the United States, shall, on board of any vessel of war which at the time of its arrival within the United States was fitted and equipped as such vessel of war, enlist or enter himself, or hire or retain another subject or citizen of the same belligerent who is transiently within the United States to enlist or enter himself, to serve such belligerent on board such vessel of war, if the United States shall then be at peace with such belligerent.)

8. Fitting out and arming, or attempting to fit out and arm, or procuring to be fitted out and armed, or knowingly being concerned in the furnishing, fitting out, or arming of any ship or vessel with intent that such ship or vessel shall be employed in the service of either of the said belligerents.

9. Issuing or delivering a commission within the territory or jurisdiction of the United States for any ship or vessel to the intent that she may be employed as aforesaid.

10. Increasing or augmenting, or procuring to be increased or augmented, or knowingly being concerned in increasing or augmenting, the force of any ship of war, cruiser, or other armed vessel which at the time of her arrival within the United States was a ship of war, cruiser, or armed vessel in the service of either of the said belligerents, or belonging to the subjects or citizens of either, by adding to the number of guns of such vessel, or by changing those on board of her for guns of a larger caliber, or by the addition thereto of any equipment solely applicable to war.

11. Beginning or setting on foot or providing or preparing the means for any military expedition or enterprise to be carried on from the territory or jurisdiction of the United States against the territories or dominions of either of the said belligerents.

And I do further declare and proclaim that by the nineteenth article of the treaty of amity and commerce which was concluded between His Majesty the King of Prussia and the United States of America on the 11th day of July, A.D. 1799, which article was revived by the treaty of May 1, A.D. 1828, between the same parties, and is still in force, it was agreed that "the vessels of war, public and private, of both parties shall carry freely, wheresoever they please, the vessels and effects taken from their enemies, without being obliged to pay any duties, charges, or fees to officers of admiralty, of the customs, or any others; nor shall such prizes be arrested, searched, or put under legal process when they come to and enter the ports of the other party, but may freely be carried out again at any time by their captors to the places expressed in their commissions, which the commanding officer of such vessel shall be obliged to show.''

And I do further declare and proclaim that it has been officially communicated to the Government of the United States by the envoy extraordinary and minister plenipotentiary of the North German Confederation at Washington that private property on the high seas will be exempted from seizure by the ships of His Majesty the King of Prussia, without regard to reciprocity.

And I do further declare and proclaim that it has been officially communicated to the Government of the United States by the envoy extraordinary and minister plenipotentiary of His Majesty the Emperor of the French at Washington that orders have been given that in the conduct of the war the commanders of the French forces on land and on the seas shall scrupulously observe toward neutral powers the rules of international law and that they shall strictly adhere to the principles set forth in the declaration of the congress of Paris of the 16th of April, 1856; that is to say:

First. That privateering is and remains abolished.

Second. That the neutral flag covers enemy's goods, with the exception of contraband of war.

Third. That neutral goods, with the exception of contraband of war, are not liable to capture under the enemy's flag.

Fourth. That blockades, in order to be binding, must be effective—that is to say, maintained by a force sufficient really to prevent access to the coast of the enemy; and that, although the United States have not adhered to the declaration of 1856, the vessels of His Majesty will not seize enemy's property found on board of a vessel of the United States, provided that property is not contraband of war.

And I do further declare and proclaim that the statutes of the United States and the law of nations alike require that no person within the territory and jurisdiction of the United States shall take part, directly or indirectly, in the said war, but shall remain at peace with each of the said belligerents and shall maintain a strict and impartial neutrality, and that whatever privileges shall be accorded to one belligerent within the ports of the United States shall be in like manner accorded to the other.

And I do hereby enjoin all the good citizens of the United States and all persons residing or being within the territory or jurisdiction of the United States, to observe the laws thereof and to commit no act contrary to the provisions of the said statutes or in violation of the law of nations in that behalf.

And I do hereby warn all citizens of the United States and all persons residing or being within their territory or jurisdiction that while the free and full expression of sympathies in public and private is not restricted by the laws of the United States, military forces in aid of either belligerent can not lawfully be originated or organized within their jurisdiction; and that while all persons may lawfully and without restriction, by reason of the aforesaid state of war, manufacture and sell within the United States arms and munitions of war and other articles ordinarily known as "contraband of war," yet they can not carry such articles upon the high seas for the use or service of either belligerent, nor can they transport soldiers and officers of either, or attempt to break any blockade which may be lawfully established and maintained during the war, without incurring the risk of hostile capture and the penalties denounced by the law of nations in that behalf.

And I do hereby give notice that all citizens of the United States and others who may claim the protection of this Government who may misconduct themselves in the premises will do so at their peril, and that they can in no wise obtain any protection from the Government of the United States against the consequences of their misconduct.

In witness whereof I have hereunto set my hand and caused the seal of the United States to be affixed.

(SEAL) Done at the city of Washington, this 22d day of August, A.D. 1870, and of the Independence of the United States of America the ninety-fifth.

U. S. GRANT

By the President:

HAMILTON FISH, *Secretary of State*

SECOND ANNUAL MESSAGE
December 5, 1870

Although the treaty of annexation of Santo Domingo had been resoundingly defeated in the Senate the previous June, Grant in this message leaped back to the attack with a glowing description of the republic as a desirable acquisition.

To the Senate and House of Representatives:

A year of peace and general prosperity to this nation has passed since the last assembling of Congress. We have, through a kind Providence, been blessed with abundant crops, and have been spared from complications and war with foreign nations. In our midst comparative harmony has been restored. It is to be regretted, however, that a free exercise of the elective franchise has by violence and intimidation been denied to citizens in exceptional cases in several of the States lately in rebellion, and the verdict of the people has thereby been reversed. The States of Virginia, Mississippi, and Texas have been restored to representation in our national councils. Georgia, the only State now without representation, may confidently be expected to take her place there also at the beginning of the new year, and then, let us hope, will be completed the work of reconstruction. . . .

Soon after the existing war broke out in Europe the protection of the United States minister in Paris was invoked in favor of North Germans domiciled in French territory. . . .

I deemed it prudent, in view of persons of German and French birth living in the United States, to issue, soon after official notice of a state of war had been received from both belligerents, a proclamation defining the duties of the United States as a neutral and the obligations of persons residing within their territory to observe their laws and the laws of nations. . . .

It is not understood that the condition of the insurrection in Cuba has materially changed since the close of the last session of Congress. . . .

The long-deferred peace conference between Spain and the allied South American Republics has been inaugurated in Washington under the auspices of the United States. . . .

The allied and other Republics of Spanish origin on this continent may see in this fact a new proof of our sincere interest in their welfare, of our desire to see them blessed with good governments, capable of maintaining order and of preserving their respective territorial integrity, and of our sincere wish to extend our own commercial and social relations with them. The time is not probably far distant when, in the natural course of events, the European political connection with this continent will cease. Our policy should be shaped, in view of this probability, so as to ally the commercial interests of the Spanish American States more closely to our own, and thus give the United States all the preeminence and all the advantage which Mr. Monroe, Mr. Adams, and Mr. Clay contemplated when they proposed to join in the congress of Panama.

During the last session of Congress a treaty for the annexation of the Republic of San Domingo to the United States failed to receive the requisite two-thirds vote of the Senate. I was thoroughly convinced then that the best interests of this country, commercially and materially, demanded its ratification. Time has only confirmed me in this view. I now firmly believe that the moment it is known that the United States have entirely abandoned the project of accepting as a part of its territory the island of San Domingo a free port will be negotiated for by European nations in the Bay of Samana. A large commercial city will spring up, to which we will be tributary without receiving corresponding benefits, and then will be seen the folly of our rejecting so great a prize. The Government of San Domingo has voluntarily sought this annexation. It is a weak power, numbering probably less than 120,000 souls, and yet possessing one of the richest territories under the sun, capable of supporting a population of 10,000,000 people in luxury. The people of San Domingo are not capable of maintaining themselves in their present condition, and must look for outside support. They yearn for the protection of our free institutions and laws, our progress and civilization. Shall we refuse them?

The acquisition of San Domingo is desirable because of its geographical position. It commands the entrance to the Caribbean Sea and the Isthmus transit of commerce. It possesses the richest soil, best and most capacious harbors, most salubrious climate, and the most valuable products of the forests, mine, and soil of any of the West India Islands. Its possession by us will in a few years build up a coastwise commerce of immense magnitude, which will go far toward restoring to us our lost merchant marine. It will give to us those articles which we consume so largely and do not produce, thus equalizing our exports and imports. In case of foreign war it will give us command of all the islands referred to, and thus prevent an enemy from ever again possessing himself of rendezvous upon our very coast. At present our coast trade between the States bordering on the Atlantic and those bordering on the Gulf of Mexico is cut into by the Bahamas and the Antilles. Twice we must, as it were, pass through foreign countries to get by sea from Georgia to the west coast of Florida.

San Domingo, with a stable government, under which her immense resources can be developed, will give remunerative wages to tens of thousands of laborers not now upon the island. This labor will take advantage of every available means of transportation to abandon the adjacent islands and seek the blessings of freedom and its sequence—each inhabitant receiving the reward of his own labor. Porto Rico and Cuba will have to abolish slavery, as a measure of self-preservation, to retain their laborers.

San Domingo will become a large consumer of the products of Northern farms and manufactories. The cheap rate at which her citizens can be furnished with food, tools, and machinery will make it necessary that contiguous islands should have the same advantages in order to compete in the production of sugar, coffee, tobacco, tropical fruits, etc. This will open to us a still wider market for our products. The production of our own supply of these articles will cut off more than one hundred millions of our annual imports, besides largely increasing our exports. With such a picture it is easy to see how our large debt abroad is ultimately to be extinguished. With a balance of trade against us (including interest on bonds held by foreigners and money spent by our citizens traveling in foreign lands) equal to the entire yield of the precious metals in this country, it is not so easy to see how this result is to be otherwise accomplished.

The acquisition of San Domingo is an adherence to the "Monroe Doctrine"; it is a measure of national protection; it is asserting our just claim to a controlling influence over the great commercial traffic soon to flow from west to east by way of the Isthmus of Darien; it is to build up our merchant marine; it is to furnish new markets for the products of our farms, shops, and manufactories; it is to make slavery insupportable in Cuba and Porto Rico at once, and ultimately so in Brazil; it is to settle the unhappy condition of Cuba and end an exterminating conflict; it is to provide honest means of paying our honest debts without overtaxing the people; it is to furnish our citizens with the necessaries of everyday life at cheaper rates than ever before; and it is, in fine, a rapid stride toward that greatness which the intelligence, industry, and enterprise of the citizens of the United States entitle this country to assume among nations.

In view of the importance of this question, I earnestly urge upon Congress early action expressive of its views as to the best means of acquiring San Domingo. My suggestion is that by joint resolution of the two Houses of Congress the Executive be authorized to appoint a commission to negotiate a treaty with the authorities of San Domingo for the acquisition of that island, and that an appropriation be made to defray the expenses of such a commission. The question may then be determined, either by the action of the Senate upon the treaty or the joint action of the two Houses of Congress upon a resolution of annexation, as in the case of the acquisition of Texas. So convinced am I of the advantages to flow from the acquisition of San Domingo, and of the great disadvantages—I might almost say calamities—to flow from nonacquisition, that I believe the subject has only to be investigated to be approved. . . .

I regret to say that no conclusion has been reached for the adjustment of the claims against Great Britain growing out of the course adopted by that Government during the rebellion. . . .

The course pursued by the Canadian authorities toward the fishermen of the United States during the past season has not been marked by a friendly feeling. . . . Vessels have been seized without notice or warning, in violation of the custom previously prevailing, and have been taken into the colonial ports, their voyages broken up, and the vessels condemned. There is reason to believe that this unfriendly and vexations treatment was designed to bear harshly upon the hardy fishermen of the United States, with a view to political effect upon this Government. . . .

Anticipating that an attempt may possibly be made by the Canadian authorities in the coming season to repeat their unneighborly acts toward our fishermen, I recommend you to confer upon the Executive the power to suspend by proclamation the operation of the laws authorizing the transit of goods, wares, and merchandise in bond across the territory of the United States to Canada, and, further, should such an extreme measure become necessary, to suspend the operation of any laws whereby the vessels of the Dominion of Canada are permitted to enter the waters of the United States.

A like unfriendly disposition has been manifested on the part of Canada in the maintenance of a claim of right to exclude the citizens of the United States from the navigation of the St. Lawrence. . . .

The whole nation is interested in securing cheap transportation from the agricultural States of the West to the Atlantic Seaboard. To the citizens of those States it secures a greater return for their labor; to the inhabitants of the seaboard it affords cheaper food; to the nation, an increase in the annual surplus of wealth. It is hoped that the Government of Great Britain will see the justice of abandoning the narrow and inconsistent claim to which her Canadian Provinces have urged her adherence. . .

The cost of building iron vessels, the only ones that can compete with foreign ships in the carrying trade, is so much greater in the United States than in foreign countries that without some assistance from the Government they can not be successfully built here. There will be several propositions laid before Congress in the course of the present session looking to a remedy for this evil. Even if it should be at some cost to the National Treasury, I hope such encouragement will be given as will secure American shipping on the high seas and American shipbuilding at home. . . .

Always favoring practical reforms, I respectfully call your attention to one abuse of long standing which I would like to see remedied by this Congress. It is a reform in the civil service of the country. I would have it go beyond the mere fixing of the tenure of office of clerks and employees who do not require "the advice and consent of the Senate" to make their appointments complete. I would have it govern, not the tenure, but the manner of making all appointments. There is no duty which so much embarrasses the Executive and heads of Departments as that of appointments, nor is there any such arduous and thankless labor imposed on Senators and Representatives as that of finding places for constituents. The present system does not secure the best men, and often not even fit men, for public place. The elevation and purification of the civil service of the Government will be hailed with approval by the whole people of the United States.

Reform in the management of Indian affairs has received the special attention of the Administration from its inauguration to the present day. The experiment of making it a missionary work was tried with a few agencies given to the denomination of Friends, and has been found to work most advantageously. All agencies and superintendencies not so disposed of were given to officers of the Army. The act of Congress reducing the Army renders army officers ineligible for civil positions. Indian agencies being civil offices, I determined to give all the agencies to such religious denominations as had heretofore established missionaries among the Indians, and perhaps to some other denominations who would undertake the work on the same terms— *i.e.,* as a missionary work. The societies selected are allowed to name their own agents, subject to the approval of the Executive, and are expected to watch over them and aid them as missionaries, to Christianize and civilize the Indian, and to train him in the arts of peace. The Government watches over the official acts of these agents, and requires of them as strict an accountability as if they were appointed in any other manner. I entertain the confident hope that the policy now pursued will in a few years bring all the Indians upon reservations, where they will live in houses, and have schoolhouses and churches, and will be pursuing peaceful and self-sustaining avocations, and where they may be visited by the law-abiding white man with the same impunity that he now visits the civilized white settlements. . . .

During the last fiscal year 8,095,413 acres of public land were disposed of. Of this quantity 3,698,910.05 acres were taken under the homestead law and 2,159,515.81 acres sold for cash. The remainder was located with military warrants, college or Indian scrip, or applied in satisfaction of grants to railroads or for other public uses. . . .

The subjects of education and agriculture are of great interest to the success of our republican institutions, happiness, and grandeur as a nation. In the interest of one a bureau has been established in the Interior Department—the Bureau of Education; and in the interest of the other, a separate Department, that of Agriculture: I believe great general good is to flow from the operations of both these Bureaus if properly fostered. I can not commend to your careful consideration too highly the reports of the Commissioners of Education and of Agriculture, nor urge too strongly such liberal legislation as to secure their efficiency.

In conclusion I would sum up the policy of the Administration to be a thorough enforcement of every law; a faithful collection of every tax provided for; economy in the disbursement of the same; a prompt payment of every debt of the nation; a reduction of taxes as rapidly as the requirements of the country will admit; reductions of taxation and tariff, to be so arranged as to afford the greatest relief to the greatest number; honest and fair dealings with all other peoples, to the end that war, with all its blighting consequences, may be avoided, but without surrendering any right or obligation due to us; a reform in the treatment of Indians and in the whole civil service of the country; and, finally, in securing a pure, untrammeled ballot, where every man entitled to cast a vote may do do so, just once at each election, without fear of molestation or proscription on account of his political faith, nativity, or color.

ON THE ANNEXATION REPORT
April 5, 1871

The bitterness aroused by the debates on annexation of the Dominican Republic is reflected in this Presidential message to Congress.

EXECUTIVE MANSION, April 5, 1871

To the Senate and House of Representatives:

I have the honor to submit herewith to the two Houses of Congress the report of the commissioners appointed in pursuance of joint resolution approved January 12, 1871.

It will be observed that this report more than sustains all that I have heretofore said in regard to the productiveness and healthfulness of the Republic of San Domingo, of the unanimity of the people for annexation to the United States, and of their peaceable character.

It is due to the public, as it certainly is to myself, that I should here give all the circumstances which first led to the negotiation of a treaty for the annexation of the Republic of San Domingo to the United States.

When I accepted the arduous and responsible position which I now hold, I did not dream of instituting any steps for the acquisition of insular possessions. I believed, however, that our institutions were broad enough to extend over the entire continent as rapidly as other peoples might desire to bring themselves under our protection. I believed further that we should not permit any independent government within the limits of North America to pass from a condition of independence to one of ownership or protection under a European power.

Soon after my inauguration as President I was waited upon by an agent of President Baez with a proposition to annex the Republic of San Domingo to the United States. This gentleman represented the capacity of the island, the desire of the people, and their character and habits about as they have been described by the commissioners whose report accompanies this message. He stated further that, being weak in numbers and poor in purse, they were not capable of developing their great resources; that the people had no incentive to industry on account of lack of protection for their accumulations, and that if not accepted by the United States—with institutions which they loved above those of any other nation—they would be compelled to seek protection elsewhere. To these statements I made no reply and gave no indication of what I thought of the proposition. In the course of time I was waited upon by a second gentleman from San Domingo, who made the same representations, and who was received in like manner.

In view of the facts which had been laid before me, and with an earnest desire to maintain the "Monroe doctrine," I believed that I would be derelict in my duty if I did not take measures to ascertain the exact wish of the Government and inhabitants of the Republic of San Domingo in regard to annexation and communicate the information to the people of the United States. Under the attending circumstances I felt that if I turned a deaf ear to this appeal I might in the future be justly charged with a flagrant neglect of the public interests and an utter disregard of the welfare of a downtrodden race praying for the blessings of a free and strong government and for protection in the enjoyment of the fruits of their own industry.

Those opponents of annexation who have heretofore professed to be preeminently the friends of the rights of man I believed would be my most violent assailants if I neglected so clear a duty. Accordingly, after having appointed a commissioner to visit the island, who declined on account of sickness, I selected a second gentleman, in whose capacity, judgment, and integrity I had, and have yet, the most unbounded confidence.

He visited San Domingo, not to secure or hasten annexation, but, unprejudiced and unbiased, to learn all the facts about the Government, the people, and the resources of that Republic. He went certainly as well prepared to make an unfavorable report as a favorable one, if the facts warranted it. His report fully corroborated the views of previous commissioners, and upon its receipt I felt that a sense of duty and a due regard for our great national interests required me to negotiate a treaty or the acquisition of the Republic of San Domingo.

As soon as it became publicly known that such a treaty had been negotiated, the attention of the country was occupied with allegations calculated to prejudice the merits of the case and with aspersions upon those whose duty had connected them with it. Amid the public excitement thus created the treaty failed to receive the requisite two-thirds vote of the Senate, and was rejected; but whether the action of that body was based wholly upon the merits of the treaty, or might not have been in some degree influenced by such unfounded allegations, could not be known by the people, because the debates of the Senate in secret session are not published.

Under these circumstances I deemed it due to the office which I hold and due to the character of the agents who had been charged with the investigation that such proceedings should be had as would enable the people to know the truth. A commission was therefore constituted, under authority of Congress, consisting of gentlemen selected with special reference to their high character and capacity for the laborious work intrusted to them, who were instructed to visit the spot and report upon the facts. Other eminent citizens were requested to accompany the commission, in order that the people might have the benefit of their views. Students of science and correspondents of the press, without regard to political opinions, were invited to join the expedition, and their numbers were limited only by the capacity of the vessel.

The mere rejection by the Senate of a treaty negotiated by the President only indicates a difference of opinion between two coordinate departments of the Government, without touching the character or wounding the pride of either. But when such rejection takes place simultaneously with charges openly made of corruption on the part of the President or those employed by him the case is different. Indeed, in such case the honor of the nation demands investigation. This has been accomplished by the report of the commissioners herewith transmitted, and which fully vindicates the purity of the motives and action of those who represented the United States in the negotiation.

And now my task is finished, and with it ends all personal solicitude upon the subject. My duty being done, yours begins; and I gladly hand over the whole matter to the judgment of the American people and of their representatives in Congress assembled. The facts will now be spread before the country, and a decision rendered by that tribunal whose convictions so seldom err, and against whose will I have no policy to enforce. My opinion remains unchanged; indeed, it is confirmed by the report that the interests of our country and of San Domingo alike invite the annexation of that Republic.

In view of the difference of opinion upon this subject, I suggest that no action be taken at the present session beyond the printing and general dissemination of the report. Before the next session of Congress the people will have considered the subject and formed an intelligent opinion concerning it, to which opinion, deliberately made up, it will be the duty of every department of the Government to give heed; and no one will more cheerfully conform to it than myself. It is not only the theory of our Constitution that the will of the people, constitutionally expressed, is the supreme law, but I have ever believed that "all men are wiser than any one man;" and if the people, upon a full presentation of the facts, shall decide that the annexation of the Republic is not desirable, every department of the Government ought to acquiesce in that decision.

In again submitting to Congress a subject upon which public sentiment has been divided, and which has been made the occasion of acrimonious debates in Congress, as well as of unjust aspersions elsewhere, I may, I trust, be indulged in a single remark.

No man could hope to perform duties so delicate and responsible as pertain to the Presidential office without sometimes incurring the hostility of those who deem their opinions and wishes treated with insufficient consideration; and he who undertakes to conduct the affairs of a great government as a faithful public servant, if sustained by the approval of his own conscience, may rely with confidence upon the candor and intelligence of a free people whose best interests he has striven to subserve, and can bear with patience the censure of disappointed men.

A PROCLAMATION
May 3, 1871

The Ku Klux Klan Bill of April 20, 1871, was to lead
to massive arrests in the South by Federal authorities,
as indicated by the following proclamations.

The act of Congress entitled "An act to enforce the provisions of the fourteenth amendment to the Constitution of the United States, and for other purposes," approved April 20, A.D. 1871, being a law of extraordinary public importance, I consider it my duty to issue this my proclamation, calling the attention of the people of the United States thereto, enjoining upon all good citizens, and especially upon all public officers, to be zealous in the enforcement thereof, and warning all persons to abstain from committing any of the acts thereby prohibited.

This law of Congress applies to all parts of the United States and will be enforced everywhere to the extent of the powers vested in the Executive. But inasmuch as the necessity therefor is well known to have been caused chiefly by persistent violations of the rights of citizens of the United States by combinations of lawless and disaffected persons in certain localities lately the theater of insurrection and military conflict, I do particularly exhort the people of those parts of the country to suppress all such combinations by their own voluntary efforts through the agency of local laws and to maintain the rights of all citizens of the United States and to secure to all such citizens the equal protection of the laws.

Fully sensible of the responsibility imposed upon the Executive by the act of Congress to which public attention is now called, and reluctant to call into exercise any of the extraordinary powers thereby conferred upon me except in cases of imperative necessity, I do, nevertheless, deem it my duty to make known that I will not hesitate to exhaust the powers thus vested in the Executive whenever and wherever it shall become necessary to do so for the purpose of securing to all citizens of the United States the peaceful enjoyment of the rights guaranteed to them by the Constitution and laws.

It is my earnest wish that peace and cheerful obedience to law may prevail throughout the land and that all traces of our late unhappy civil strife may be speedily removed. These ends can be easily reached by acquiescence in the results of the conflict, now written in our Constitution, and by the due and proper enforcement of equal, just, and impartial laws in every part of our country.

The failure of local communities to furnish such means for the attainment of results so earnestly desired imposes upon the National Government the duty of putting forth all its energies for the protection of its citizens of every race and color and for the restoration of peace and order throughout the entire country.

In testimony whereof I have hereunto set my hand and caused the seal of the United States to be affixed.

(SEAL)   Done at the city of Washington, this 3d day of May, A.D. 1871, and of the Independence of the United States the ninety-fifth.

U. S. GRANT

By the President:
HAMILTON FISH,
Secretary of State

A PROCLAMATION
October 12, 1871

Whereas unlawful combinations and conspiracies have long existed and do still exist in the State of South Carolina for the purpose of depriving certain portions and classes of the people of that State of the rights, privileges, immunities, and protection named in the Constitution of the United States and secured by the act of Congress approved April 20, 1871, entitled "An act to enforce the provisions of the fourteenth amendment to the Constitution of the United States," and

Whereas in certain parts of said State, to wit, in the counties of Spartanburg, York, Marion, Chester, Laurens, Newberry, Fairfield, Lancaster, and Chesterfield, such combinations and conspiracies do so obstruct and hinder the execution of the laws of said State and of the United States as to deprive the people aforesaid of the rights, privileges, immunities, and protection aforesaid and do oppose and obstruct the laws of the United States and their due execution and impede and obstruct the due course of justice under the same; and

Whereas the constituted authorities of said State are unable to protect the people aforesaid in such rights within the said counties; and

Whereas the combinations and conspiracies aforesaid, within the counties aforesaid, are organized and armed and are so numerous and powerful as to be able to defy the constituted authorities of said State and of the United States within the said State, and by reason of said causes the conviction of such offenders and the preservation of the public peace and safety have become impracticable in said counties:

Now, therefore, I, Ulysses S. Grant, President of the United States of America, do hereby command all persons composing the unlawful combinations and conspiracies aforesaid to disperse and to retire peaceably to their homes within five days of the date hereof, and to deliver either to the marshal of the United States for the district of South Carolina, or to any of his deputies, or to any military officer of the United States within said counties, all arms, ammunition, uniforms, disguises, and other means and implements used, kept, possessed, or controlled by them for carrying out the unlawful purposes for which the combinations and conspiracies are organized.

In witness whereof I have hereunto set my hand and caused the seal of the United States to be affixed.

(SEAL)   Done at the city of Washington, this 12th day of October, A.D. 1871, and of the Independence of the United States of America the ninety-sixth.

U. S. GRANT

By the President:
     HAMILTON FISH,
         Secretary of State

A PROCLAMATION
October 17, 1871

Whereas by an act of Congress entitled "An act to enforce the provisions of the fourteenth amendment to the Constitution of the United States, and for other purposes," approved the 20th day of April, A.D. 1871, power is given to the President of the United States, when in his judgment the public safety shall require it, to suspend the privileges of the writ of *habeas corpus* in any State or part of a State whenever combinations and conspiracies exist in such State or part of a State for the purpose of depriving any portion or class of the people of such State of the rights, privileges, immunities, and protection named in the Constitution of the United States and secured by the act of Congress aforesaid; and whenever such combinations and conspiracies do so obstruct and hinder the execution of the laws of any such State and of the United States as to deprive the people aforesaid of the rights, privileges, immunities, and protection aforesaid, and do oppose and obstruct the laws of the United States and their due execution, and impede and obstruct the due course or justice under the same; and whenever such combinations shall be organized and armed, and so numerous and powerful as to be able by violence either to overthrow or to set at defiance the constituted authorities of said State and of the United States within such State; and whenever by reason of said causes the conviction of such offenders and the preservation of the public peace shall become in such State or part of a State impracticable; and

Whereas such unlawful combinations and conspiracies for the purposes aforesaid are declared by the act of Congress aforesaid to be rebellion against the Government of the United States; and

Whereas by said act of Congress it is provided that before the President shall suspend the privileges of the writ of *habeas corpus* he shall first have made proclamation commanding such insurgents to disperse; and

Whereas on the 12th day of the present month of October the President of the United States did issue his proclamation, reciting therein, among other things, that such combinations and conspiracies did then exist in the counties of Spartanburg, York, Marion, Chester, Laurens, Newberry, Fairfield, Lancaster, and Chesterfield, in the State of South Carolina, and commanding thereby all persons composing such unlawful combinations and conspiracies to disperse and retire peaceably to their homes within five days from the date thereof, and to deliver either to the marshal of the United States for the district of South Carolina, or to any of his deputies, or to any military officer of the United States within said counties, all arms, ammunition, uniforms, disguises, and other means and implements used, kept, possessed, or controlled by them for carrying out the unlawful purposes for which the said combinations and conspiracies are organized; and

Whereas the insurgents engaged in such unlawful combinations and conspiracies within the counties aforesaid have not dispersed and retired peaceably to their respective homes, and have not delivered to the marshal of the United States, or to any of his deputies, or to any military officer of the United States within said counties, all arms, ammunition, uniforms, disguises, and other means and implements used, kept, possessed, or controlled by them for carrying out the unlawful purposes for which the combinations and conspiracies are organized, as commanded by said proclamation, but do still persist in the unlawful combinations and conspiracies aforesaid:

Now, therefore, I, Ulysses S. Grant, President of the United States of America, by virtue of the authority vested in me by the Constitution of the United States and the act of Congress aforesaid, do hereby declare that in my judgment the public safety especially requires that the privileges of the writ of *habeas corpus* be suspended, to the end that such rebellion may be overthrown, and do hereby suspend the privileges of the writ of *habeas corpus* within the counties of Spartanburg, York, Marion, Chester, Laurens, Newberry, Fairfield, Lancaster, and Chesterfield, in said State of South Carolina, in respect to all persons arrested by the marshal of the United States for the said district of South Carolina, or by any of his deputies, or by any military officer of the United States, or by any soldier or citizen acting under the orders of said marshal, deputy, or such military officer within any one of said counties, charged with any violation of the act of Congress aforesaid, during the continuance of such rebellion.

In witness whereof I have hereunto set my hand ane caused the seal of the United States to be affixed.

(SEAL) Done at the city of Washington, this 17th day of October, A.D. 1871, and of the Independence of the United States of America the ninety-sixth.

By the President: J. C. BANCROFT DAVIS,
Acting Secretary of State

A PROCLAMATION
November 3, 1871

Whereas in my proclamation of the 12th day of October, in the year 1871, it was recited that certain unlawful combinations and conspiracies existed in certain counties in the State of South Carolina for the purpose of depriving certain portions and classes of the people of that State of the rights, privileges, and immunities and protection named in the Constitution of the United States and secured by the act of Congress approved April 20, 1871, entitled "An act to enforce the provisions of the four-teenth amendment to the Constitution of the United States," and the persons composing such combinations and conspiracies were commanded to disperse and to retire peaceably to their homes within five days from said date; and

Whereas by my proclamation of the 17th day of October, in the year 1871, the privileges of the writ of *habeas corpus* were suspended in the counties named in said proclamation; and

Whereas the county of Marion was named in said proclamations as one of the counties in which said unlawful combinations and conspiracies for the purposes aforesaid existed, and in which the privileges of the writ of *habeas corpus* were suspended; and

Whereas it has been ascertained that in said county of Marion said combinations and conspiracies do not exist to the extent recited in said proclamations; and

Whereas it has been ascertained that unlawful combinations and con-spiracies of the character and to the extent and for the purposes described in said proclamations do exist in the county of Union in said State:

Now, therefore, I, Ulysses S. Grant, President of the United States of America, do hereby revoke, as to the said county of Marion, the suspension of the privileges of the writ of *habeas corpus* directed in my said proclamation of the 17th day of October, 1871.

And I do hereby command all persons in the said county of Union composing the unlawful combinations and conspiracies aforesaid to dis-perse and to retire peaceably to their homes within five days of the date hereof, and to deliver either to the marshal of the United States for the district of South Carolina, or to any of his deputies, or to any military officer of the United States within said county, all arms, ammunition, uniforms, disguises, and other means and implements used, kept, pos-sessed, or controlled by them for carrying out the unlawful purposes for which the combinations and conspiracies are organized.

In witness whereof I have hereunto set my hand and caused the seal of the United States to be affixed.

(SEAL)   Done at the city of Washington, this 3d day of November, A.D. 1871, and of the Independence of the United States of America the ninety-sixth.

By the President: HAMILTON FISH,
Secretary of State

THIRD ANNUAL MESSAGE
December 4, 1871

This message reflects Grant's satisfaction with the successful settlement of the long standing "Alabama claims" dispute. It also contains one of his many pleas for civil service reform.

To the Senate and House of Representatives:

In addressing my third annual message to the law-making branch of the Government it is gratifying to be able to state that during the past year success has generally attended the effort to execute all laws found upon the statute books. The policy has been not to inquire into the wisdom of laws already enacted, but to learn their spirit and intent and to enforce them accordingly.

The past year has, under a wise Providence, been one of general prosperity to the nation. . . .

The relations of the United States with foreign powers continue to be friendly. The year has been an eventful one in witnessing two great nations, speaking one language and having one lineage, settling by peaceful arbitration disputes of long standing and liable at any time to bring those nations into bloody and costly conflict. . . .

I transmit herewith a copy of the treaty alluded to, which has been concluded since the adjournment of Congress with Her Britannic Majesty, and a copy of the protocols of the conferences of the commissioners by whom it was negotiated. This treaty provides methods for adjusting the questions pending between the two nations.

Various questions are to be adjusted by arbitration. I recommend Congress at an early day to make the necessary provision for the tribunal at Geneva and for the several commissioners on the part of the United States called for by the treaty. . . .

The Forty-first Congress, at its third session, made an appropriation for the organization of a mixed commission for adjudicating upon the claims of citizens of the United States against Spain growing out of the insurrection in Cuba. That commission has since been organized. . . .

It has been made the agreeable duty of the United States to preside over a conference at Washington between the plenipotentiaries of Spain and the allied South American Republics, which has resulted in an armistice, with the reasonable assurance of a permanent peace.

The intimate friendly relations which have so long existed between the United States and Russia continue undisturbed. . . .

It is to be regretted that the disturbed condition of the island of Cuba continues to be a source of annoyance and of anxiety. . . .

Our naval commanders in Cuban waters have been instructed, in case it should become necessary, to spare no effort to protect the lives and property of *bona fide* American citizens and to maintain the dignity of the flag. . . .

The national debt has been reduced to the extent of $86,057,126.80 during the year, and by the negotiation of national bonds at a lower rate of interest the interest on the public debt has been so far diminished that now the sum to be raised for the interest account is nearly $17,000,000 less than on the 1st of March, 1869. It was highly desirable that this rapid diminution should take place, both to strengthen the credit of the country and to convince its citizens of their entire ability to meet every dollar of liability without bankrupting them. But in view of the accomplishment of these desirable ends: of the rapid development of the resources of the country; its increasing ability to meet large demands, and the amount already paid, it is not desirable that the present resources of the country should continue to be taxed in order to continue this rapid payment. I therefore recommend a modification of both the tariff and internal-tax law. I recommend that all taxes from internal sources be abolished, except those collected from spirituous, vinous, and malt liquors, tobacco in its various forms, and from stamps. . . .

Continued fluctuations in the value of gold, as compared with the national currency, has a most damaging effect upon the increase and development of the country, in keeping up prices of articles necessary in everyday life. It fosters a spirit of gambling, prejudicial alike to national morals and the national finances. If the question can be met as to how to get a fixed value to our currency, that value constantly and uniformly approaching par with specie, a very desirable object will be gained. . . .

There has been imposed upon the executive branch of the Government the execution of the act of Congress approved April 20, 1871, and commonly known as the Kuklux law, in a portion of the State of South Carolina. The necessity of the course pursued will be demonstrated by the report of the Committee to Investigate Southern Outrages. Under the provisions of the above act I issued a proclamation calling the attention of the people of the United States to the same, and declaring my reluctance to exercise any of the extraordinary powers thereby conferred upon me, except in case of imperative necessity, but making known my purpose to exercise such powers whenever it should become necessary to do so for the purpose of securing to all citizens of the United States the peaceful enjoyment of the rights guaranteed to them by the Constitution and the laws.

After the passage of this law information was received from time to time that combinations of the character referred to in this law existed and were powerful in many parts of the Southern States, particularly in certain counties in the State of South Carolina.

Careful investigation was made, and it was ascertained that in nine counties of that State such combinations were active and powerful, embracing a sufficient portion of the citizens to control the local authority, and having, among other things, the object of depriving the emancipated class of the substantial benefits of freedom and of preventing the free political action of those citizens who did not sympathize with their own views. Among their operations were frequent scourgings and occasional assassinations, generally perpetrated at night by disguised persons, the victims in almost all cases being citizens of different political sentiments from their own or freed persons who had shown a disposition to claim equal rights with other citizens. Thousands of inoffensive and well-disposed citizens were the sufferers by this lawful violence.

Thereupon, on the 12th of October, 1871, a proclamation was issued, in terms of the law, calling upon the members of those combinations to disperse within five days and to deliver to the marshal or military officers of the United States all arms, ammunition, uniforms, disguises, and other means and implements used by them for carrying out their unlawful purposes.

This warning not having been heeded, on the 17th of October another proclamation was issued, suspending the privileges of the writ of *habeas corpus* in nine counties in that State.

Direction was given that within the counties so designated persons supposed, upon creditable information, to be members of such unlawful combinations should be arrested by the military forces of the United States and delivered to the marshal, to be dealt with according to law. In two of said counties, York and Spartanburg, many arrests have been made. At the last account the number of persons thus arrested was 168. Several hundred, whose criminality was ascertained to be of an inferior degree, were released for the present. These have generally made confessions of their guilt.

Great caution has been exercised in making these arrests, and, not-withstanding the large number, it is believed that no innocent person is now in custody. The prisoners will be held for regular trial in the judicial tribunals of the United States. . . .

In Utah there still remains a remnant of barbarism, repugnant to civi-lization, to decency, and to the laws of the United States. Territorial officers, however, have been found who are willing to perform their duty in a spirit of equity and with a due sense of the necessity of sustaining the majesty of the law. Neither polygamy nor any other violation of existing statutes will be permitted within the territory of the United States. It is not with the religion of the self-styled Saints that we are now dealing, but with their practices. They will be protected in the worship of God according to the dictates of their consciences, but they will not be per-mitted to violate the laws under the cloak of religion. . . .

More than six years having elapsed since the last hostile gun was fired between the armies then arrayed against each other—one for the per-petuation, the other for the destruction, of the Union—it may well be considered whether it is not now time that the disabilities imposed by the fourteenth amendment should be removed. That amendment does not exclude the ballot, but only imposes the disability to hold offices upon certain classes. When the purity of the ballot is secure, majorities are sure to elect officers reflecting the views of the majority. I do not see the advantage or propriety of excluding men from office merely because they were before the rebellion of standing and character sufficient to be elected to positions requiring them to take oaths to support the Constitution, and admitting to eligibility those entertaining precisely the same views, but of less standing in their communities. It may be said that the former violated an oath, while the latter did not; the latter did not have it in their power to do so. If they had taken this oath, it can not be doubted they would have broken it as did the former class. If there are any great criminals, distinguished above all others for the part they took in opposition to the Government, they might, in the judgment of Congress, be excluded from such an amnesty. . . .

Under the provisions of the act of Congress approved February 21, 1871, a Territorial government was organized in the District of Columbia. Its results have thus far fully realized the expectations of its advocates. . . .

By the great fire in Chicago the most important of the Government buildings in that city were consumed. Those burned had already become inadequate to the wants of the Government in that growing city, and, looking to the near future, were totally inadequate. I recommend, therefore, that an appropriation be made immediately to purchase the remainder of the square on which the burned buildings stood, provided it can be purchased at a fair valuation, or provided that the legislature of Illinois will pass a law authorizing its condemnation for Government purposes; and also an appropriation of as much money as can properly be expended toward the erection of new buildings during this fiscal year.

The number of immigrants ignorant of our laws, habits, etc., coming into our country annually has become so great and the impositions practiced upon them so numerous and flagrant that I suggest Congressional action for their protection. . . .

It has been the aim of the Administration to enforce honesty and efficiency in all public offices. Every public servant who has violated the trust placed in him has been proceeded against with all the rigor of the law. If bad men have secured places, it has been the fault of the system established by law and custom for making appointments, or the fault of those who recommend for Government positions persons not sufficiently well known to them personally, or who give letters indorsing the characters of office seekers without a proper sense of the grave responsibility which such a course devolves upon them. A civil-service reform which can correct this abuse is much desired. In mercantile pursuits the business man who gives a letter of recommendation to a friend to enable him to obtain credit from a stranger is regarded as morally responsible for the integrity of his friend and his ability to meet his obligations. A reformatory law which would enforce this principle against all indorsers of persons for public place would insure great caution in making recommendations. A salutary lesson has been taught the careless and the dishonest public servant in the great number of prosecutions and convictions of the last two years.

It is gratifying to notice the favorable change which is taking place throughout the country in bringing to punishment those who have proven recreant to the trusts confided to them and in elevating to public office none but those who possess the confidence of the honest and the virtuous, who, it will always be found, comprise the majority of the community in which they live.

In my message to Congress one year ago I urgently recommended a reform in the civil service of the country. In conformity with that recommendation Congress, in the ninth section of "An act making appropriations for sundry civil expenses of the Government, and for other purposes," approved March 3, 1871, gave the necessary authority to the Executive to inaugurate a civil-service reform, and placed upon him the responsibility of doing so. Under the authority of said act I convened a board of gentlemen eminently qualified for the work to devise rules and regulations to effect the needed reform. Their labors are not yet complete, but it is believed that they will succeed in devising a plan that can be adopted to the great relief of the Executive, the heads of Departments, and members of Congress, and which will redound to the true interest of the public service. At all events, the experiment shall have a fair trial. . . .

ON KLAN VIOLENCE
April 19, 1872

The depth of the Klan-perpetrated terror is clear from this message of Grant to the House.

EXECUTIVE MANSION, April 19, 1872

To the House of Representatives:

In answer to the resolution of the House of Representatives of the 25th of January last, I have the honor to submit the following, accompanied by the report of the Attorney-General, to whom the resolution was referred:

Representations having been made to me that in certain portions of South Carolina a condition of lawlessness and terror existed, I requested the then Attorney-General (Akerman) to visit that State, and after personal examination to report to me the facts in relation to the subject. On the 16th of October last he addressed me a communication from South Carolina, in which he stated that in the counties of Spartanburg, York, Chester, Union, Laurens, Newberry, Fairfield, Lancaster, and Chesterfield there were combinations for the purpose of preventing the free political action of citizens who were friendly to the Constitution and the Government of the United States, and of depriving emancipated classes of the equal protection of the laws.

"These combinations embrace at least two-thirds of the active white men of those counties, and have the sympathy and countenance of a majority of the one-third. They are connected with similar combinations in other counties and States, and no doubt are part of a grand system of criminal associations pervading most of the Southern States. The members are bound to obedience and secrecy by oaths which they are taught to regard as of higher obligation than the lawful oaths taken before civil magistrates.

"They are organized and armed. They effect their objects by personal violence, often extending to murder. They terrify witnesses; they control juries in the State courts, and sometimes in the courts of the United States. Systematic perjury is one of the means by which prosecutions of the members are defeated. From information given by officers of the State and of the United States and by credible private citizens I am justified in affirming that the instances of criminal violence perpetrated by these combinations within the last twelve months in the above-named counties could be reckoned by thousands."

I received information of a similar import from various other sources, among which were the Joint Select Committee of Congress upon Southern Outrages, the officers of the State, the military officers of the United States on duty in South Carolina, the United States attorney and marshal, and other civil officers of the Government, repentant and abjuring members of those unlawful organizations, persons specially employed by the Department of Justice to detect crimes against the United States, and from other credible persons.

Most, if not all, of this information, except what I derived from the Attorney-General, came to me orally, and was to the effect that said counties were under the sway of powerful combinations, properly known as "Kuklux Klans," the objects of which were by force and terror to prevent all political action not in accord with the views of the members; to deprive colored citizens of the right to bear arms and of the right to a free ballot; to suppress schools in which colored children were taught, and to reduce the colored people to a condition closely akin to that of slavery; that these combinations were organized and armed, and had rendered the local laws ineffectual to protect the classes whom they desired to oppress; that they had perpetrated many murders and hundreds of crimes of minor degree, all of which were unpunished; and that witnesses could not safely testify against them unless the more active members were placed under restraint.

FOURTH ANNUAL MESSAGE
December 2, 1872

In this final annual message of his first term as President, Grant in his comments on disorders in the South reflects the strong enforcement policy of his Administration.

To the Senate and House of Representatives:

In transmitting to you this my fourth annual message it is with thankfulness to the Giver of All Good that as a nation we have been blessed for the past year with peace at home, peace abroad, and a general prosperity vouchsafed to but few peoples. . . .

When Congress adjourned in June last, a question had been raised by Great Britain, and was then pending, which for a time seriously imperiled the settlement by friendly arbitration of the grave differences between this Government and that of Her Britannic Majesty, which by the treaty of Washington had been referred to the tribunal of arbitration which had met at Geneva, in Switzerland.

The arbitrators, however, disposed of the question which had jeoparded the whole of the treaty and threatened to involve the two nations in most unhappy relations toward each other in a manner entirely satisfactory to this Government and in accordance with the views and the policy which it had maintained.

The tribunal, which had convened at Geneva in December, concluded its laborious session on the 14th day of September last, on which day, having availed itself of the discretionary power given to it by the treaty to award a sum in gross, it made its decision, whereby it awarded the sum of $15,500,000 in gold as the indemnity to be paid by Great Britain to the United States for the satisfaction of all the claims referred to its consideration.

This decision happily disposes of a long-standing difference between the two Governments, and, in connection with another award, made by the German Emperor under a reference to him by the same treaty, leaves these two Governments without a shadow upon the friendly relations which it is my sincere hope may forever remain equally unclouded. . . .

By the thirty-fourth article of the treaty of Washington the respective claims of the United States and of Great Britain in their construction of the treaty of the 15th of June, 1846, defining the boundary line between their respective territories, were submitted to the arbitration and award of His Majesty the Emperor of Germany, to decide which of those claims is most in accordance with the true interpretation of the treaty of 1846. . . .

After a patient investigation of the case and of the statements of each party, His Majesty the Emperor, on the 21st day of October last, signed his award in writing. . . .

This award confirms the United States in their claim to the important archipelago of islands lying between the continent and Vancouvers Island, which for more than twenty-six years (ever since the ratification of the treaty) Great Britain has contested, and leaves us, for the first time in the history of the United States as a nation, without a question of disputed boundary between our territory and the possessions. of Great Britain on this continent. . . .

In my last annual message I recommended the legislation necessary on the part of the United States to bring into operation the articles of the treaty of Washington of May 8, 1871, relating to the fisheries and to other matters touching the relations of the United States toward the British North American possessions, to become operative so soon as the proper legislation should be had on the part of Great Britain and its possessions.

That legislation on the part of Great Britain and its possessions had not then been had, and during the session of Congress a question was raised which for the time raised a doubt whether any action by Congress in the direction indicated would become important. This question has since been disposed of, and I have received notice that the Imperial Parliament and the legislatures of the provincial governments have passed laws to carry the provisions of the treaty on the matters referred to into operation. I therefore recommend your early adoption of the legislation in the same direction necessary on the part of this Government. . . .

It is much to be regretted that many lawless acts continue to disturb the quiet of the settlements on the border between our territory and that of Mexico, and that complaints of wrongs to American citizens in various parts of the country are made. The revolutionary condition in which the neighboring Republic has so long been involved has in some degree contributed to this disturbance. It is to be hoped that with a more settled rule of order through the Republic, which may be expected from the present Government, the acts of which just complaint is made will cease.

The proceedings of the commission under the convention with Mexico of the 4th of July, 1868, on the subject of claims, have, unfortunately, been checked by an obstacle, for the removal of which measures have been taken by the two Governments which it is believed will prove successful.

The commissioners appointed, pursuant to the joint resolution of Congress of the 7th of May last, to inquire into depredations on the Texan frontier have diligently made investigations in that quarter. Their report upon the subject will be communicated to you. Their researches were necessarily incomplete, partly on account of the limited appropriation made by Congress. Mexico, on the part of that Government, has appointed a similar commission to investigate these outrages. It is not announced officially, but the press of that country states that the fullest investigation is desired, and that the cooperation of all parties concerned is invited to secure that end. I therefore recommend that a special appropriation be made at the earliest day practicable, to enable the commissioners on the part of the United States to return to their labors without delay.

It is with regret that I have again to announce a continuance of the disturbed condition of the island of Cuba. . . .

I can not doubt that the continued maintenance of slavery in Cuba is among the strongest inducements to the continuance of this strife. A terrible wrong is the natural cause of a terrible evil. . . .

Reckless and lawless men, I regret to say, have associated themselves together in some localities to deprive other citizens of those rights guaranteed to them by the Constitution of the United States, and to that end have committed deeds of blood and violence; but the prosecution and punishment of many of these persons have tended greatly to the repression of such disorders. . . .

Applications have been made to me to pardon persons convicted of a violation of such acts, upon the ground that clemency in such cases would tend to tranquilize the public mind, and to test the virtue of that policy I am disposed, as far as my sense of justice will permit, to give to these applications a favorable consideration; but any action thereon is not to be construed as indicating any change in my determination to enforce with vigor such acts so long as the conspiracies and combinations therein named disturb the peace of the country. . . .

The subject of converting the so-called Indian Territory south of Kansas into a home for the Indians, and erecting therein a Territorial form of government, is one of great importance as a complement of the existing Indian policy. . . . Efforts will be made in the immediate future to induce the removal of as many peaceably disposed Indians to the Indian Territory as can be settled properly without disturbing the harmony of those already there. . . . A Territorial government should, however, protect the Indians from the inroads of whites for a term of years, until they become sufficiently advanced in the arts and civilization to guard their own rights, and from the disposal of the lands held by them for the same period. . . .

In accordance with the terms of the act of Congress approved March 3, 1871, providing for the celebration of the one hundredth anniversary of American independence, a commission has been organized. . . .

This celebration will be looked forward to by American citizens with great interest, as marking a century of greater progress and prosperity than is recorded in the history of any other nation. . . .

An earnest desire has been felt to correct abuses which have grown up in the civil service of the country through the defective method of making appointments to office. . . . During my term of office it shall be my earnest endeavor to so apply the rules as to secure the greatest possible reform in the civil service of the Government. . . .

ON UTAH COURTS
February 14, 1873

This urgent recommendation for legislation to strengthen the Federal courts in Utah reflects the turmoil incident to Federal enforcement of the anti-polygamy law of 1862.

EXECUTIVE MANSION, February 14, 1873

To the Senate and House of Representatives:

I consider it my duty to call the attention of Congress to the condition of affairs in the Territory of Utah, and to the dangers likely to arise if it continues during the coming recess, from a threatened conflict between the Federal and Territorial authorities.

No discussion is necessary in regard to the general policy of Congress respecting the Territories of the United States, and I only wish now to refer to so much of that policy as concerns their judicial affairs and the enforcement of law within their borders.

No material differences are found in respect to these matters in the organic acts of the Territories, but an examination of them will show that it has been the invariable policy of Congress to place and keep their civil and criminal jurisdiction, with certain limited exceptions, in the hands of persons nominated by the President and confirmed by the Senate, and that the general administration of justice should be as prescribed by Congressional enactment. Sometimes the power given to the Territorial legislatures has been somewhat larger and sometimes somewhat smaller than the powers generally conferred. Never, however, have powers been given to a Territorial legislature inconsistent with the idea that the general judicature of the Territory was to be under the direct supervision of the National Government.

Accordingly, the organic law creating the Territory of Utah, passed September 9, 1850, provided for the appointment of a supreme court, the judges of which are judges of the district courts, a clerk, marshal, and an attorney, and to these Federal officers is confided jurisdiction in all important matters; but, as decided recently by the Supreme Court, the act requires jurors to serve in these courts to be selected in such manner as the territorial legislature sees fit to prescribe. It has undoubtedly been the desire of Congress, so far as the same might be compatible with the supervisory control of the Territorial government, to leave the minor details connected with the administration of law to regulation by local authority; but such a desire ought not to govern when the effect will be, owing to the peculiar circumstances of the case, to produce a conflict between the Federal and the Territorial authorities, or to impede the enforcement of law, or in any way to endanger the peace and good order of the Territory.

Evidently it was never intended to intrust the Territorial legislature with power which would enable it, by creating judicatures of its own or increasing the jurisdiction of courts appointed by Territorial authority, although recognized by Congress, to take the administration of the law out of the hands of the judges appointed by the President or to interfere with their action.

Several years of unhappy experience make it apparent that in both of these respects the Territory of Utah requires special legislation by Congress.

Public opinion in that Territory, produced by circumstances too notorious to require further notice, makes it necessary, in my opinion, in order to prevent the miscarriage of justice and to maintain the supremacy of the laws of the United States and of the Federal Government, to provide that the selection of grand and petit jurors for the district courts, if not put under the control of Federal officers, shall be placed in the hands of persons entirely independent of those who are determined not to enforce any act of Congress obnoxious to them, and also to pass some act which shall deprive the probate courts, or any court created by the Territorial legislature, of any power to interfere with or impede the action of the courts held by the United States judges.

I am convinced that so long as Congress leaves the selection of jurors to the local authorities it will be futile to make any effort to enforce laws not acceptable to a majority of the people of the Territory, or which interfere with local prejudices or provide for the punishment of polygamy or any of its affiliated vices or crimes.

I presume that Congress, in passing upon the subject, will provide all reasonable and proper safeguards to secure honest and impartial jurors, whose verdicts will command confidence and be a guaranty of equal protection to all good and law-abiding citizens, and at the same time make it understood that crime can not be committed with impunity.

I have before said that while the laws creating the several Territories have generally contained uniform provisions in respect to the judiciary, yet Congress has occasionally varied these provisions in minor details, as the circumstances of the Territory affected seemed to demand; and in creating the Territory of Utah Congress evidently thought that circumstances there might require judicial remedies not necessary in other Territories, for by section 9 of the act creating that Territory it is provided that a writ of error may be brought from the decision of any judge of the supreme or district court of the Territory to the Supreme Court of the United States upon any writ of *habeas corpus* involving the question of personal freedom—a provision never inserted in any other Territorial act except that creating the Territory of New Mexico.

This extraordinary provision shows that Congress intended to mold the organic law to the peculiar necessities of the Territory, and the legislation which I now recommend is in full harmony with the precedent thus established.

I am advised that United States courts in Utah have been greatly embarrassed by the action of the Territorial legislature in conferring criminal jurisdiction and the power to issue writs of *habeas corpus* on the probate courts in the Territory, and by their consequent interference with the administration of justice. Manifestly the legislature of the Territory can not give to any court whatever the power to discharge by *habeas corpus* persons held by or under process from the courts created by Congress, but complaint is made that persons so held have been discharged in that way by the probate courts. I can not doubt that Congress will agree with me that such a state of things ought not longer to be tolerated, and that no class of persons anywhere should be allowed to treat the laws of the United States with open defiance and contempt.

Apprehensions are entertained that if Congress adjourns without any action upon this subject turbulence and disorder will follow, rendering military interference necessary—a result I should greatly deprecate; and in view of this and other obvious considerations, I earnestly recommend that Congress, at the present session, pass some act which will enable the district courts of Utah to proceed with independence and efficiency in the administration of law and justice.

SECOND INAUGURAL ADDRESS
March 4, 1873

This compendium of generalities drew the scornful arrows of the press.

FELLOW-CITIZENS: Under Providence I have been called a second time to act as Executive over this great nation. It has been my endeavor in the past to maintain all the laws, and, so far as lay in my power, to act for the best interests of the whole people. My best efforts will be given in the same direction in the future, aided, I trust, by my four years' experience in the office.

When my first term of the office of Chief Executive began, the country had not recovered from the effects of a great internal revolution, and three of the former States of the Union had not been restored to their Federal relations.

It seemed to me wise that no new questions should be raised so long as that condition of affairs existed. Therefore the past four years, so far as I could control events, have been consumed in the effort to restore harmony, public credit, commerce, and all the arts of peace and progress. It is my firm conviction that the civilized world is tending toward republicanism, or government by the people through their chosen representatives, and that our own great Republic is destined to be the guiding star to all others.

Under our Republic we support an army less than that of any European power of any standing and a navy less than that of either of at least five of them. There could be no extension of territory on the continent which would call for an increase of this force, but rather might such extension enable us to diminish it.

The theory of government changes with general progress. Now that the telegraph is made available for communicating thought, together with rapid transit by steam, all parts of a continent are made contiguous for all purposes of government, and communication between the extreme limits of the country made easier than it was throughout the old thirteen States at the beginning of our national existence.

The effects of the late civil strife have been to free the slave and make him a citizen. Yet he is not possessed of the civil rights which citizenship should carry with it. This is wrong, and should be corrected. To this correction I stand committed, so far as Executive influence can avail.

Social equality is not a subject to be legislated upon, nor shall I ask that anything be done to advance the social status of the colored man, except to give him a fair chance to develop what there is good in him, give him access to the schools, and when he travels let him feel assured that his conduct will regulate the treatment and fare he will receive.

The States lately at war with the General Government are now happily rehabilitated, and no Executive control is exercised in any one of them that would not be exercised in any other State under like circumstances.

In the first year of the past Administration the proposition came up for the admission of Santo Domingo as a Territory of the Union. It was not a question of my seeking, but was a proposition from the people of Santo Domingo, and which I entertained. I believe now, as I did then, that it was for the best interest of this country, for the people of Santo Domingo, and all concerned that the proposition should be received favorably. It was, however, rejected constitutionally, and therefore the subject was never brought up again by me.

In future, while I hold my present office, the subject of acquisition of territory must have the support of the people before I will recommend any proposition looking to such acquisition. I say here, however, that I do not share in the apprehension held by many as to the danger of governments becoming weakened and destroyed by reason of their extension of territory. Commerce, education, and rapid transit of thought and matter by telegraph and steam have changed all this. Rather do I believe that our Great Maker is preparing the world, in His own good time, to become one nation, speaking one language, and when armies and navies will be no longer required.

My efforts in the future will be directed to the restoration of good feeling between the different sections of our common country; to the restoration of our currency to a fixed value as compared with the world's standard of values—gold—and, if possible, to a par with it; to the construction of cheap routes of transit throughout the land, to the end that the products of all may find a market and leave a living remuneration to the producer; to the maintenance of friendly relations with all our neighbors and with distant nations; to the reestablishment of our commerce and share in the carrying trade upon the ocean; to the encouragement of such manufacturing industries as can be economically pursued in this country, to the end that the exports of home products and industries may pay for our imports—the only sure method of returning to and permanently maintaining a specie basis; to the elevation of labor; and, by a humane course, to bring the aborigines of the country under the benign influences of education and civilization. It is either this or war of extermination. Wars of extermination, engaged in by people pursuing commerce and all industrial pursuits, are expensive even against the weakest people, and are demoralizing and wicked. Our superiority of strength and advantages of civilization should make us lenient toward the Indian. The wrong inflicted upon him should be taken into account and the balance placed to his credit. The moral view of the question should be considered and the question asked, Can not the Indian be made a useful and productive member of society by proper teaching and treatment? If the effort is made in good faith, we will stand better before the civilized nations of the earth and in our consciences for having made it.

All these things are not to be accomplished by one individual, but they will receive my support and such recommendations to Congress as will in my judgment best serve to carry them into effect. I beg your support and encouragement.

It has been, and is, my earnest desire to correct abuses that have grown up in the civil service of the country. To secure this reformation rules regulating methods of appointment and promotions were established and have been tried. My efforts for such reformation shall be continued to the best of my judgment. The spirit of the rules adopted will be maintained.

I acknowledge before this assemblage, representing, as it does, every section of our country, the obligation I am under to my countrymen for the great honor they have conferred on me by returning me to the highest office within their gift, and the further obligation resting on me to render to them the best services within my power. This I promise, looking forward with the greatest anxiety to the day when I shall be released from responsibilities that at times are almost overwhelming, and from which I have scarcely had a respite since the eventful firing upon Fort Sumter, in April, 1861, to the present day. My services were then tendered and accepted under the first call for troops growing out of that event.

I did not ask for place or position, and was entirely without influence or the acquaintance of persons of influence, but was resolved to perform my part in a struggle threatening the very existence of the nation. I performed a conscientious duty, without asking promotion or command, and without a revengeful feeling toward any section or individual.

Notwithstanding this, throughout the war, and from my candidacy for my present office in 1868 to the close of the last Presidential campaign, I have been the subject of abuse and slander scarcely ever equaled in political history, which to-day I feel that I can afford to disregard in view of your verdict, which I gratefully accept as my vindication.

FIFTH ANNUAL MESSAGE
December 1, 1873

A few days before Grant delivered this message to Congress, the diplomatic efforts of Secretary of State Hamilton Fish had resolved the Virginius *affair, thus abating the war fever and enabling the President to open his annual report happily.*

To the Senate and House of Representatives:

The year that has passed since the submission of my last message to Congress has, especially during the latter part of it, been an eventful one to the country. In the midst of great national prosperity a financial crisis has occurred that has brought low fortunes of gigantic proportions; political partisanship has almost ceased to exist, especially in the agricultural regions; and, finally, the capture upon the high seas of a vessel bearing our flag has for a time threatened the most serious consequences, and has agitated the public mind from one end of the country to the other. But this, happily, now is in the course of satisfactory adjustment, honorable to both nations concerned. . . .

I transmit herewith, for the consideration and determination of Congress, an application of the Republic of Santo Domingo to this Government to exercise a protectorate over that Republic.

Since the adjournment of Congress the following treaties with foreign powers have been proclaimed: A naturalization convention with Denmark; a convention with Mexico for renewing the Claims Commission; a convention of friendship, commerce, and extradition with the Orange Free State, and a naturalization convention with Ecuador.

I renew the recommendation made in my message of December, 1870, that Congress authorize the Postmaster-General to issue all commissions to officials appointed through his Department.

I invite the earnest attention of Congress to the existing laws of the United States respecting expatriation and the election of nationality by individuals. . . .

. . . I invite Congress now to mark out and define when and how expatriation can be accomplished; to regulate by law the condition of American women marrying foreigners; to fix the status of children born in a foreign country of American parents residing more or less permanently abroad, and to make rules for determining such other kindred points as may seem best to Congress. . . .

The steamer *Virginius* was on the 26th day of September, 1870, duly registered at the port of New York as a part of the commercial marine of the United States. On the 4th of October, 1870, having received the certificate of her register in the usual legal form, she sailed from the port of New York and has not since been within the territorial jurisdiction of the United States. On the 31st day of October last, while sailing under the flag of the United States on the high seas, she was forcibly seized by the Spanish gunboat *Tornado,* and was carried into the port of Santiago de Cuba, where fifty-three of her passengers and crew were inhumanly, and so far at least as relates to those who were citizens of the United States, without due process of law, put to death.

It is a well-established principle, asserted by the United States from the beginning of their national independence, recognized by Great Britain and other maritime powers, and stated by the Senate in a resolution passed unanimously on the 16th of June, 1858, that—

> American vessels on the high seas in time of peace, bearing the American flag, remain under the jurisdiction of the country to which they belong, and therefore any visitation, molestation, or detention of such vessel by force, or by the exhibition of force, on the part of a foreign power is in derogation of the sovereignty of the United States.

In accordance with this principle, the restoration of the *Virginius* and the surrender of the survivors of her passengers and crew, and a due reparation to the flag, and the punishment of the authorities who had been guilty of the illegal acts of violence, were demanded. The Spanish Government has recognized the justice of the demand, and has arranged for the immediate delivery of the vessel, and for the surrender of the survivors of the passengers and crew, and for a salute to the flag, and for proceedings looking to the punishment of those who may be proved to have been guilty of illegal acts of violence toward citizens of the United States, and also toward indemnifying those who may be shown to be entitled to indemnity. . . .

The embargoing of American estates in Cuba, cruelty to American citizens detected in no act of hostility to the Spanish Government, the murdering of prisoners taken with arms in their hands, and, finally, the capture upon the high seas of a vessel sailing under the United States flag and bearing a United States registry have culminated in an outburst of indignation that has seemed for a time to threaten war. Pending negotiations between the United States and the Government of Spain on the subject of this capture, I have authorized the Secretary of the Navy to put our Navy on a war footing, to the extent, at least, of the entire annual appropriation for that branch of the service, trusting to Congress and the public opinion of the American people to justify my action. . . .

The revenues have materially fallen off for the first five months of the present fiscal year from what they were expected to produce, owing to the general panic now prevailing. . . .

My own judgment is that, however much individuals may have suffered, one long step has been taken toward specie payments; that we can never have permanent prosperity until a specie basis is reached. . . .

The experience of the present panic has proven that the currency of the country, based, as it is, upon the credit of the country, is the best that has ever been devised. . . .

With the encroachment of civilization upon the Indian reservations and hunting grounds, disturbances have taken place between the Indians and whites during the past year, and probably will continue to do so until each race appreciates that the other has rights which must be respected.

The policy has been to collect the Indians as rapidly as possible on reservations, and as far as practicable within what is known as the Indian Territory, and to teach them the arts of civilization and self-support. Where found off their reservations, and endangering the peace and safety of the whites, they have been punished, and will continue to be for like offenses.

The Indian Territory south of Kansas and west of Arkansas is sufficient in area and agricultural resources to support all the Indians east of the Rocky Mountains. In time, no doubt, all of them, except a few who may elect to make their homes among white people, will be collected there. As a preparatory step for this consummation, I am now satisfied that a Territorial form of government should be given them, which will secure the treaty rights of the original settlers and protect their homesteads from alienation for a period of twenty years. . . .

In three successive messages to Congress I have called attention to the subject of "civil-service reform."

Action has been taken so far as to authorize the appointment of a board to devise rules governing methods of making appointments and promotions, but there never has been any action making these rules, or any rules, binding, or even entitled to observance, where persons desire the appointment of a friend or the removal of an official who may be disagreeable to them.

To have any rules effective they must have the acquiescence of Congress as well as of the Executive. I commend, therefore, the subject to your attention, and suggest that a special committee of Congress might confer with the Civil-Service Board during the present session for the purpose of devising such rules as can be maintained, and which will secure the services of honest and capable officials, and which will also protect them in a degree of independence while in office. . . .

I would recommend for your favorable consideration the passage of an enabling act for the admission of Colorado as a State in the Union. It possesses all the elements of a prosperous State, agricultural and mineral, and, I believe, has a population now to justify such admission. In connection with this I would also recommend the encouragement of a canal for purposes of irrigation from the eastern slope of the Rocky Mountains to the Missouri River. . . .

I renew my previous recommendation to Congress for general amnesty. The number engaged in the late rebellion yet laboring under disabilities is very small, but enough to keep up a constant irritation. No possible danger can accrue to the Government by restoring them to eligibility to hold office.

I suggest for your consideration the enactment of a law to better secure the civil rights which freedom should secure, but has not effectually secured, to the franchised slave.

VETO OF INFLATION ACT
April 22, 1874

There was general expectation that Grant would approve this act. Influenced by Secretary of State Fish, who feared even further inflationary actions, Grant reversed his position.

To the Senate of the United States:

Herewith I return Senate bill No. 617, entitled "An act to fix the amount of United States notes and the circulation of national banks, and for other purposes," without my approval.

In doing so I must express my regret at not being able to give my assent to a measure which has received the sanction of a majority of the legislators chosen by the people to make laws for their guidance, and I have studiously sought to find sufficient arguments to justify such assent, but unsuccessfully.

Practically it is a question whether the measure under discussion would give an additional dollar to the irredeemable paper currency of the country or not, and whether by requiring three-fourths of the reserve to be retained by the banks and prohibiting interest to be received on the balance it might not prove a contraction.

But the fact can not be concealed that theoretically the bill increases the paper circulation $100,000,000, less only the amount of reserves restrained from circulation by the provision of the second section. The measure has been supported on the theory that it would give increased circulation. It is a fair inference, therefore, that if in practice the measure should fail to create the abundance of circulation expected of it the friends of the measure, particularly those out of Congress, would clamor for such inflation as would give the expected relief.

The theory, in my belief, is a departure from true principles of finance, national interest, national obligations to creditors, Congressional promises, party pledges (on the part of both political parties), and of personal views and promises made by me in every annual message sent to Congress and in each inaugural address.

In my annual message to Congress in December, 1869, the following passages appear:

> Among the evils growing out of the rebellion, and not yet referred to, is that of an irredeemable currency. It is an evil which I hope will receive your most earnest attention. It is a duty, and one of the highest duties, of Government to secure to the citizen a medium of exchange of fixed, unvarying value. This implies a return to a specie basis, and no substitute for it can be devised. It should be commenced now and reached at the earliest practicable moment consistent with a fair regard to the interests of the debtor class. Immediate resumption, if practicable, would not be desirable. It would compel the debtor class to pay, beyond their contracts, the premium on gold at the date of their purchase, and would bring bankruptcy and ruin to thousands. Fluctuation, however, in the paper value of the measure of all values (gold) is detrimental to the interests of trade. It makes the man of business an involuntary gambler, for in all sales where future payment is to be made both parties speculate as to what will be the value of the currency to be paid and received. I earnestly recommend to you, then, such legislation as will insure a gradual return to specie payments and put an immediate stop to fluctuations in the value of currency.

I still adhere to the views then expressed.

As early as December 4, 1865, the House of Representatives passed a resolution, by a vote of 144 yeas to 6 nays, concurring "in the views of the Secretary of the Treasury in relation to the necessity of a contraction of the currency, with a view to as early a resumption of specie payments as the business interests of the country will permit," and pledging "cooperative action to this end as speedily as possible."

The first act passed by the Forty-first Congress, (approved) on the 18th day of March, 1869, was as follows:

AN ACT to strengthen the public credit.

Be it enacted, etc., That in order to remove any doubt as to the purpose of the Government to discharge all just obligations to the public creditors, and to settle conflicting questions and interpretations of the law by virtue of which such obligations have been contracted, it is hereby provided and declared that the faith of the United States is solemnly pledged to the payment in coin or its equivalent of all the obligations of the United States not bearing interest, known as United States notes, and all the interest-bearing obligations of the United States, except in cases where the law authorizing the issue of such obligation has expressly provided that the same may be paid in lawful money or in other currency than gold and silver; but none of the said interest-bearing obligations not already due shall be redeemed or paid before maturity unless at such time United States notes shall be convertible into coin at the option of the holder, or unless at such time bonds of the United States bearing a lower rate of interest than the bonds to be redeemed can be sold at par in coin. And the United States also solemnly pledges its faith to make provision at the earliest practicable period for the redemption of the United States notes in coin.

This act still remains as a continuing pledge of the faith of the United States "to make provision at the earliest practicable period for the redemption of the United States notes in coin."

A declaration contained in the act of June 30, 1864, created an obligation that the total amount of United States notes issued or to be issued should never exceed $400,000,000. The amount in actual circulation was actually reduced to $356,000,000, at which point Congress passed the act of February 4, 1868, suspending the further reduction of the currency. The forty-four millions have ever been regarded as a reserve, to be used only in case of emergency, such as has occurred on several occasions, and must occur when from any cause revenues suddenly fall below expenditures; and such a reserve is necessary, because the fractional currency, amounting to fifty millions, is redeemable in legal tender on call.

It may be said that such a return of fractional currency for redemption is impossible; but let steps be taken for a return to a specie basis and it will be found that silver will take the place of fractional currency as rapidly as it can be supplied, when the premium on gold reaches a sufficiently low point. With the amount of United States notes to be issued permanently fixed within proper limits and the Treasury so strengthened as to be able to redeem them in coin on demand it will then be safe to inaugurate a system of free banking with such provisions as to make compulsory redemption of the circulating notes of the banks in coin, or in United States notes, themselves redeemable and made equivalent to coin.

As a measure preparatory to free banking, and for placing the Government in a condition to redeem its notes in coin "at the earliest practicable period," the revenues of the country should be increased so as to pay current expenses, provide for the sinking fund required by law, and also a surplus to be retained in the Treasury in gold.

I am not a believer in any artificial method of making paper money equal to coin when the coin is not owned or held ready to redeem the promises to pay, for paper money is nothing more than promises to pay, and is valuable exactly in proportion to the amount of coin that it can be converted into. While coin is not used as a circulating medium, or the currency of the country is not convertible into it at par, it becomes an article of commerce as much as any other product. The surplus will seek a foreign market as will any other surplus. The balance of trade has nothing to do with the question. Duties on imports being required in coin creates a limited demand for gold. About enough to satisfy that demand remains in the country. To increase this supply I see no way open, but by the Government hoarding through the means above given, and possibly by requiring the national banks to aid.

It is claimed by the advocates of the measure herewith returned that there is an unequal distribution of the banking capital of the country. I was disposed to give great weight to this view of the question at first, but on reflection it will be remembered that there still remains $4,000,000 of authorized bank-note circulation assigned to States having less than their quota not yet taken. In addition to this the States having less than their quota of bank circulation have the option of twenty-five millions more to be taken from those States having more than their proportion. When this is all taken up, or when specie payments are fully restored or are in rapid process of restoration, will be the time to consider the question of "more currency."

ON THE VIRGINIUS AFFAIR
January 5, 1874

*The President's words give some hint of the delicate
diplomacy—on the part of both countries involved—
which resolved the potentially explosive sovereignty
issue.*

To the Senate and House of Representatives:

In my annual message of December last I gave reason to expect that
when the full and accurate text of the correspondence relating to the
steamer *Virginius*, which had been telegraphed in cipher, should be
received the papers concerning the capture of the vessel, the execution
of a part of its passengers and crew, and the restoration of the ship and
the survivors would be transmitted to Congress.

In compliance with the expectations then held out, I now transmit the
papers and correspondence on that subject.

On the 26th day of September, 1870, the *Virginius* was registered in
the custom-house at New York as the property of a citizen of the United
States, he having first made oath, as required by law, that he was "the
true and only owner of the said vessel, and that there was no subject
or citizen of any foreign prince or state, directly or indirectly, by way of
trust, confidence, or otherwise, interested therein."

Having complied with the requisites of the statute in that behalf, she
cleared in the usual way for the port of Curacoa, and on or about the
4th day of October, 1870, sailed for that port. It is not disputed that she
made the voyage according to her clearance, nor that from that day to
this she has not returned within the territorial jurisdiction of the United
States. It is also understood that she preserved her American papers,
and that when within foreign ports she made the practice of putting
forth a claim to American nationality, which was recognized by the
authorities at such ports.

When, therefore, she left the port of Kingston, in October last, under
the flag of the United States, she would appear to have had, as against
all powers except the United States, the right to fly that flag and to
claim its protection, as enjoyed by all regularly documented vessels registered as part of our commercial marine.

No state of war existed conferring upon a maritime power the right to
molest and detain upon the high seas a documented vessel, and it can
not be pretended that the *Virginius* had placed herself without the pale
of all law by acts of piracy against the human race.

If her papers were irregular or fraudulent, the offense was one against
the laws of the United States, justiciable only in their tribunals.

When, therefore, it became known that the *Virginius* had been captured on the high seas by a Spanish man-of-war; that the American flag
had been hauled down by the captors; that the vessel had been carried

to a Spanish port, and that Spanish tribunals were taking jurisdiction over the persons of those found on her, and exercising that jurisdiction upon American citizens, not only in violation of the rules of international law, but in contravention of the provisions of the treaty of 1795, I directed a demand to be made upon Spain for the restoration of the vessel and for the return of the survivors to the protection of the United States, for a salute to the flag, and for the punishment of the offending parties.

The principles upon which these demands rested could not be seriously questioned, but it was suggested by the Spanish Government that there were grave doubts whether the *Virginius* was entitled to the character given her by her papers, and that therefore it might be proper for the United States, after the surrender of the vessel and the survivors, to dispense with the salute to the flag, should such fact be established to their satisfaction.

This seemed to be reasonable and just. I therefore assented to it, on the assurance that Spain would then declare that no insult to the flag of the United States had been intended.

I also authorized an agreement to be made that should it be shown to the satisfaction of this Government that the *Virginius* was improperly bearing the flag proceedings should be instituted in our courts for the punishment of the offense committed against the United States. On her part Spain undertook to proceed against those who had offended the sovereignty of the United States, or who had violated their treaty rights.

The surrender of the vessel and the survivors to the jurisdiction of the tribunals of the United States was an admission of the principles upon which our demands had been founded. I therefore had no hesitation in agreeing to the arrangement finally made between the two Governments—an arrangement which was moderate and just, and calculated to cement the good relations which have so long existed between Spain and the United States.

Under this agreement the *Virginius*, with the American flag flying, was delivered to the Navy of the United States at Bahia Honda, in the island of Cuba, on the 16th ultimo. She was then in an unseaworthy condition. In the passage to New York she encountered one of the most tempestuous of our winter storms. At the risk of their lives the officers and crew placed in charge of her attempted to keep her afloat. Their efforts were unavailing, and she sank off Cape Fear. The prisoners who survived the massacres were surrendered at Santiago de Cuba on the 18th ultimo, and reached the port of New York in safety.

The evidence submitted on the part of Spain to establish the fact that the *Virginius* at the time of her capture was improperly bearing the flag of the United States is transmitted herewith, together with the opinion of the Attorney-General thereon and a copy of the note of the Spanish minister, expressing on behalf of his Government a disclaimer of an intent of indignity to the flag of the United States.

U. S. GRANT

SIXTH ANNUAL MESSAGE
December 7, 1874

*Grant indicated the importance he attached to a re-
turn to a specie basis by launching into that subject
first. However, public attention—mostly critical—was
focused at the time on highhanded Federal intervention in politics in the South, particularly in Louisiana.*

To the Senate and House of Representatives:

Since the convening of Congress one year ago the nation has undergone
a prostration in business and industries such as has not been witnessed
with us for many years. . . . During this prostration two essential elements of prosperity have been most abundant—labor and capital. Both
have been largely unemployed . . . Debt, debt abroad, is the only element that can, with always a sound currency, enter into our affairs to
cause any continued depression in the industries and prosperity of our
people.

A great conflict for national existence made necessary, for temporary
purposes, the raising of large sums of money from whatever source at-
tainable. It made necessary, in the wisdom of Congress. . . . to devise a
system of national currency which it proved to be impossible to keep on a
par with the recognized currency of the civilized world. . . . Where a
new market can be created for the sale of our products, either of the soil,
the mine, or the manufactory, a new means is discovered of utilizing
our idle capital and labor to the advantage of the whole people. But in
my judgment, the first step toward accomplishing this object is to secure
a currency of fixed, stable value; a currency good wherever civilization
reigns . . . Gold and silver are now the recognized medium of exchange
the civilized world over, and to this we should return with the least
practicable delay. . . .

. . . But I will venture to suggest two or three things which seem to
me as absolutely necessary to a return to specie payments, the first great
requisite in a return to prosperity. The legal-tender clause to the law
authorizing the issue of currency by the National Government should be
repealed, to take effect as to all contracts entered into after a day fixed
in the repealing act . . . Provision should be made by which the Secretary of the Treasury can obtain gold as it may become necessary from
time to time from the date when specie redemption commences. To this
might and should be added a revenue sufficiently in excess of expenses
to insure an accumulation of gold in the Treasury to sustain permanent
redemption. . . .

The Secretary of the Treasury in his report favors legislation looking to
an early return to specie payments, thus supporting views previously expressed in this message. He also recommends economy in appropriations. . . .

Your attention will be drawn to the unsettled condition of affairs in some of the Southern States.

On the 14th of September last the governor of Louisiana called upon me, as provided by the Constitution and laws of the United States, to aid in suppressing domestic violence in that State. . . . On the next day I issued my proclamation commanding the insurgents to disperse within five days from the date thereof. . . .

I regret to say that with preparations for the late election decided indications appeared in some localities in the Southern States of a determination, by acts of violence and intimidation, to deprive citizens of the freedom of the ballot because of their political opinions. Bands of men, masked and armed, made their appearance; White Leagues and other societies were formed . . . the proper officers were instructed to prosecute the offenders, and troops were stationed at convenient points to aid these officers, if necessary, in the performance of their official duties. Complaints are made of this interference by Federal authority; but if said amendment and act do not provide for such interference under the circumstances as above stated, then they are without meaning, force, or effect, and the whole scheme of colored enfranchisement is worse than mockery and little better than a crime. . . .

The rules adopted to improve the civil service of the Government have been adhered to as closely as has been practicable with the opposition with which they meet. . . . But it is impracticable to maintain them without direct and positive support of Congress. Generally the support which this reform receives is from those who give it their support only to find fault when the rules are apparently departed from. Removals from office without preferring charges against parties removed are frequently cited as departures from the rules adopted, and the retention of those against whom charges are made by irresponsible persons and without good grounds is also often condemned as a violation of them. Under these circumstances, therefore, I announce that if Congress adjourns without positive legislation on the subject of "civil-service reform," I will regard such action as a disapproval of the system, and will abandon it except so far as to require examinations for certain appointees, to determine their fitness. Competitive examinations will be abandoned. . . .

A revival of shipbuilding, and particularly of iron steamship building, is of vast importance to our national prosperity. . . .

ON LOUISIANA ELECTIONS
January 13, 1875

*Grant explained use of Federal troops in supporting
the Kellogg government in Louisiana.*

To the Senate of the United States:

I have the honor to make the following answer to a Senate resolution
of the 8th instant, asking for information as to any interference by any
military officer or any part of the Army of the United States with the
organization or proceedings of the general assembly of the State of Louisiana, or either branch thereof; and also inquiring in regard to the existence of armed organizations in that State hostile to the government
thereof and intent on overturning such government by force.

To say that lawlessness, turbulence, and bloodshed have characterized
the political affairs of that State since its reorganization under the reconstruction acts is only to repeat what has become well known as a part of
its unhappy history; but it may be proper here to refer to the election
of 1868, by which the Republican vote of the State, through fraud and
violence, was reduced to a few thousands, and the bloody riots of 1866
and 1868, to show that the disorders there are not due to any recent
causes or to any late action of the Federal authorities.

Preparatory to the election of 1872 a shameful and undisguised con-
spiracy was formed to carry that election against the Republicans, without
regard to law or right, and to that end the most glaring frauds and for-
geries were committed in the returns, after many colored citizens had been
denied registration and others deterred by fear from casting their ballots.

When the time came for a final canvass of the votes, in view of the fore-
going facts William P. Kellogg, the Republican candidate for governor,
brought suit upon the equity side of the United States circuit court for
Louisiana, and against Warmoth and others, who had obtained possession
of the returns of the election, representing that several thousand voters of
the States had been deprived of the elective franchise on account of their
color, and praying that steps might be taken to have said votes counted
and for general relief. To enable the court to inquire as to the truth of
these allegations, a temporary restraining order was issued against the
defendants, which was at once wholly disregarded and treated with contempt by those to whom it was directed. These proceedings have been
widely denounced as an unwarrantable interference by the Federal judiciary with the election of State officers; but it is to be remembered that
by the fifteenth amendment to the Constitution of the United States the
political equality of colored citizens is secured, and under the second
section of that amendment, providing that Congress shall have power to
enforce its provisions by appropriate legislation, an act was passed on the

31st of May, 1870, and amended in 1871, the object of which was to prevent the denial or abridgment of suffrage to citizens on account of race, color, or previous condition of servitude; and it has been held by all the Federal judges before whom the question has arisen, including Justice Strong, of the Supreme Court, that the protection afforded by this amendment and these acts extends to State as well as other elections. That it is the duty of the Federal courts to enforce the provisions of the Constitution of the United States and the laws passed in pursuance thereof is too clear for controversy.

Section 15 of said act, after numerous provisions therein to prevent an evasion of the fifteenth amendment, provides that the jurisdiction of the circuit court of the United States shall extend to all cases in law or equity arising under the provisions of said act and of the act amendatory thereof. Congress seems to have contemplated equitable as well as legal proceedings to prevent the denial of suffrage to colored citizens; and it may be safely asserted that if Kellogg's bill in the above-named case did not present a case for the equitable interposition of the court, that no such case can arise under the act. That the courts of the United States have the right to interfere in various ways with State elections so as to maintain political equality and rights therein, irrespective of race or color, is comparatively a new, and to some seems to be a startling, idea, but it results as clearly from the fifteenth amendment to the Constitution and the acts that have been passed to enforce that amendment as the abrogation of State laws upholding slavery results from the thirteenth amendment to the Constitution. While the jurisdiction of the court in the case of Kellogg *vs.* Warmoth and others is clear to my mind, it seems that some of the orders made by the judge in that and the kindred case of Antoine were illegal. But while they are so held and considered, it is not to be forgotten that the mandate of his court had been contemptuously defied, and they were made while wild scenes of anarchy were sweeping away all restraint of law and order. Doubtless the judge of this court made grave mistakes; but the law allows the chancellor great latitude, not only in punishing those who condemn his orders and injunctions, but in preventing the consummation of the wrong which he has judicially forbidden.

Whatever may be said or thought of those matters, it was only made known to me that process of the United States court was resisted, and as said act especially provides for the use of the Army and Navy when necessary to enforce judicial process arising thereunder, I considered it my duty to see that such process was executed according to the judgment of the court.

Resulting from these proceedings, through various controversies and complications, a State administration was organized with William P. Kellogg as governor, which, in the discharge of my duty under section 4, Article IV, of the Constitution, I have recognized as the government of the State.

It has been bitterly and persistently alleged that Kellogg was not elected. Whether he was or not is not altogether certain, nor is it any more certain that his competitor, McEnery, was chosen. The election was a gigantic fraud, and there are no reliable returns of its result. Kellogg obtained possession of the office, and in my opinion has more right to it than his competitor.

On the 20th of February, 1873, the Committee on Privileges and Elections of the Senate made a report in which they say they were satisfied by testimony that the manipulation of the election machinery by Warmoth and others was equivalent to 20,000 votes; and they add that to recognize the McEnery government "would be recognizing a government based upon fraud, in defiance of the wishes and intention of the voters of the State." Assuming the correctness of the statements in this report (and they seem to have been generally accepted by the country), the great crime in Louisiana, about which so much has been said, is that one is holding the office of governor who was cheated out of 20,000 votes, against another whose title to the office is undoubtedly based on fraud and in defiance of the wishes and intentions of the voters of the State.

Misinformed and misjudging as to the nature and extent of this report, the supporters of McEnery proceeded to displace by force in some counties of the State the appointees of Governor Kellogg, and on the 13th of April, in an effort of that kind, a butchery of citizens was committed at Colfax, which in bloodthirstiness and barbarity is hardly surpassed by any acts of savage warfare.

To put this matter beyond controversy I quote from the charge of Judge Woods, of the United States circuit court, to the jury in the case of The United States *vs.* Cruikshank and others, in New Orleans in March, 1874. He said:

> In the case on trial there are many facts not in controversy. I proceed to state some of them in the presence and hearing of counsel on both sides; and if I state as a conceded fact any matter that is disputed, they can correct me.

After stating the origin of the difficulty, which grew out of an attempt of white persons to drive the parish judge and sheriff, appointees of Kellogg, from office, and their attempted protection by colored persons, which led to some fighting, in which quite a number of negroes were killed, the judge states:

> Most of those who were not killed were taken prisoners. Fifteen or sixteen of the blacks had lifted the boards and taken refuge under the floor of the court-house. They were all captured. About thirty-seven men were taken prisoners. The number is not definitely fixed. They were kept under guard until dark. They were led out, two by two, and shot. Most of the men were shot to death. A few were wounded, not mortally, and by pretending to be dead were after-

wards, during the night, able to make their escape. Among them was the Levi Nelson named in the indictment.

The dead bodies of the negroes killed in this affair were left unburied until Tuesday, April 15, when they were buried by a deputy marshal and an officer of the militia from New Orleans. These persons found fifty-nine dead bodies. They showed pistol-shot wounds, the great majority in the head, and most of them in the back of the head. In addition to the fifty-nine dead bodies found, some charred remains of dead bodies were discovered near the court-house. Six dead bodies were found under a warehouse, all shot in the head but one or two, which were shot in the breast.

The only white men injured from the beginning of these troubles to their close were Hadnot and Harris. The court-house and its contents were entirely consumed.

There is no evidence that anyone in the crowd of whites bore any lawful warrant for the arrest of any of the blacks. There is no evidence that either Nash or Cazabat, after the affair, ever demanded their offices, to which they had set up claim, but Register continued to act as parish judge and Shaw as sheriff.

These are facts in this case as I understand them to be admitted.

To hold the people of Louisiana generally responsible for these atrocities would not be just, but it is a lamentable fact that insuperable obstructions were thrown in the way of punishing these murders; and the so-called conservative papers of the State not only justified the massacre, but denounced as Federal tyranny and despotism the attempt of the United States officers to bring them to justice. Fierce denunciations ring through the country about office holding and election matters in Louisiana, while every one of the Colfax miscreants goes unwhipped of justice, and no way can be found in this boasted land of civilization and Christianity to punish the perpetrators of this bloody and monstrous crime.

Not unlike this was the massacre in August last. Several Northern young men of capital and enterprise had started the little and flourishing town of Coushatta. Some of them were Republicans and officeholders under Kellogg. They were therefore doomed to death. Six of them were seized and carried away from their homes and murdered in cold blood. No one has been punished, and the conservative press of the State denounced all efforts to that end and boldly justified the crime.

Many murders of a like character have been committed in individual cases, which can not here be detailed. For example, T. S. Crawford, judge, and P. H. Harris, district attorney, of the twelfth judicial district of the State, on their way to court were shot from their horses by men in ambush on the 8th of October, 1873; and the widow of the former, in a communication to the Department of Justice, tells a piteous tale of the persecutions of her husband because he was a Union man, and of the efforts made to screen those who had committed a crime which, to use her own language, "left two widows and nine orphans desolate."

To say that the murder of a negro or a white Republican is not considered a crime in Louisiana would probably be unjust to a great part of the people, but it is true that a great number of such murders have been committed and no one has been punished therefor; and manifestly, as to them, the spirit of hatred and violence is stronger than law.

Representations were made to me that the presence of troops in Louisiana was unnecessary and irritating to the people, and that there was no danger of public disturbance if they were taken away. Consequently early in last summer the troops were all withdrawn from the State, with the exception of a small garrison at New Orleans Barracks. It was claimed that a comparative state of quiet had supervened. Political excitement as to Louisiana affairs seemed to be dying out. But the November election was approaching, and it was necessary for party purposes that the flame should be rekindled.

Accordingly, on the 14th of September D. P. Penn, claiming that he was elected lieutenant-governor in 1872, issued an inflammatory proclamation calling upon the militia of the State to arm, assemble, and drive from power the usurpers, as he designated the officers of the State. The White Leagues, armed and ready for the conflict, promptly responded.

On the same day the governor made a formal requisition upon me, pursuant to the act of 1795 and section 4, Article IV, of the Constitution, to aid in suppressing domestic violence. On the next day I issued my proclamation commanding the insurgents to disperse within five days from the date thereof; but before the proclamation was published in New Orleans the organized and armed forces recognizing a usurping governor had taken forcible possession of the statehouse and temporarily subverted the government. Twenty or more people were killed, including a number of the police of the city. The streets of the city were stained with blood. All that was desired in the way of excitement had been accomplished, and, in view of the steps taken to repress it, the revolution is apparently, though it is believed not really, abandoned, and the cry of Federal usurpation and tyranny in Louisiana was renewed with redoubled energy. Troops had been sent to the State under this requisition of the governor, and as other disturbances seemed imminent they were allowed to remain there to render the executive such aid as might become necessary to enforce the laws of the State and repress the continued violence which seemed inevitable the moment Federal support should be withdrawn.

Prior to, and with a view to, the late election in Louisiana white men associated themselves together in armed bodies called "White Leagues," and at the same time threats were made in the Democratic journals of the State that the election should be carried against the Republicans at all hazards, which very naturally greatly alarmed the colored voters. By section 8 of the act of February 28, 1871, it is made the duty of United States marshals and their deputies at polls where votes are cast for Representatives in Congress to keep the peace and prevent any violations of the so-called enforcement acts and other offenses against the laws of the United States; and upon a requisition of the marshal of Louisiana, and in view of said armed organizations and other portentous circumstances, I caused detachments of troops to be stationed in various localities in the State, to aid him in the performance of his official duties. That there was intimidation of Republican voters at the election, notwithstanding these precautions, admits of no doubt. The following are specimens of the means used:

On the 14th of October eighty persons signed and published the following at Shreveport:

We, the undersigned, merchants of the city of Shreveport, in obedience to a request of the Shreveport Campaign Club, agree to use every endeavor to get our employees to vote the People's ticket at the ensuing election, and in the event of their refusal so to do, or in case they vote the Radical ticket, to refuse to employ them at the expiration of their present contracts.

On the same day another large body of persons published in the same place a paper in which they used the following language:

We, the undersigned, merchants of the city of Shreveport, alive to the great importance of securing good and honest government to the State, do agree and pledge ourselves not to advance any supplies or money to any planter the coming year who will give employment or rent lands to laborers who vote the Radical ticket in the coming election.

I have no information of the proceedings of the returning board for said election which may not be found in its report, which has been published; but it is a matter of public information that a great part of the time taken to canvass the votes was consumed by the arguments of lawyers, several of whom represented each party before the board. I have no evidence that the proceedings of this board were not in accordance with the law under which they acted. Whether in excluding from their count certain returns they were right or wrong is a question that depends upon the evidence they had before them; but it is very clear that the law gives them the power, if they choose to exercise it, of deciding that way, and, *prima facie,* the persons whom they return as elected are entitled to the offices for which they were candidates.

Respecting the alleged interference by the military with the organization of the legislature of Louisiana on the 4th instant, I have no knowledge or information which has not been received by me since that time and published. My first information was from the papers of the morning of the 5th of January. I did not know that any such thing was anticipated, and no orders nor suggestions were ever given to any military officer in that State upon that subject prior to the occurrence. I am well aware that any military interference by the officers or troops of the United States with the organization of the State legislature or any of its proceedings, or with any civil department of the Government, is repugnant to our ideas of government. I can conceive of no case, not involving rebellion or insurrection, where such interference by authority of the General Government ought to be permitted or can be justified. But there are circumstances connected with the late legislative imbroglio in Louisiana which seem to exempt the military from any intentional wrong in that matter. Knowing that they have been placed in Louisiana to prevent domestic violence and aid in the enforcement of the State laws, the officers and troops of the United States may well have supposed that it was their duty to act when called upon by the governor for that purpose.

Each branch of a legislative assembly is the judge of the election and qualifications of its own members; but if a mob or a body of unauthorized persons seize and hold the legislative hall in a tumultuous and riotous manner, and so prevent any organization by those legally returned as elected, it might become the duty of the State executive to interpose, if requested by a majority of the members elect, to suppress the disturbance and enable the persons elected to organize the house.

Any exercise of this power would only be justifiable under most extraordinary circumstances, and it would then be the duty of the governor to call upon the constabulary or, if necessary, the military force of the State. But with reference to Louisiana, it is to be borne in mind that any attempt by the governor to use the police force of that State at this time would have undoubtedly precipitated a bloody conflict with the White League, as it did on the 14th of September.

There is no doubt but that the presence of the United States troops upon that occasion prevented bloodshed and the loss of life. Both parties appear to have relied upon them as conservators of the public peace.

The first call was made by the Democrats, to remove persons obnoxious to them from the legislative halls; and the second was from the Republicans, to remove persons who had usurped seats in the legislature without legal certificates authorizing them to seats, and in sufficient number to change the majority.

Nobody was disturbed by the military who had a legal right at that time to occupy a seat in the legislature. That the Democratic minority of the house undertook to seize its organization by fraud and violence; that in this attempt they trampled under foot law; that they undertook to make persons not returned as elected members, so as to create a majority; that they acted under a preconcerted plan, and under false pretenses introduced into the hall a body of men to support their pretensions by force if necessary, and that conflict, disorder, and riotous proceedings followed are facts that seem to be well established; and I am credibly informed that these violent proceedings were a part of a premeditated plan to have the house organized in this way, recognize what has been called the McEnery senate, then to depose Governor Kellogg, and so revolutionize the State government.

Whether it was wrong for the governor, at the request of the majority of the members returned as elected to the house, to use such means as were in his power to defeat these lawless and revolutionary proceedings is perhaps a debatable question; but it is quite certain that there would have been no trouble if those who now complain of illegal interference had allowed the house to be organized in a lawful and regular manner. When those who inaugurate disorder and anarchy disavow such proceedings, it will be time enough to condemn those who by such means as they have prevent the success of their lawless and desperate schemes.

Lieutenant-General Sheridan was requested by me to go to Louisiana to observe and report the situation there, and, if in his opinion necessary, to assume the command, which he did on the 4th instant, after the legislative disturbances had occurred, at 9 o'clock p.m., a number of hours after the disturbances. No party motives nor prejudices can reasonably be imputed to him; but honestly convinced by what he has seen and heard there, he has characterized the leaders of the White Leagues in severe terms and suggested summary modes of procedure against them, which, though they can not be adopted, would, if legal, soon put an end to the troubles and disorders in that State. General Sheridan was looking at facts, and possibly, not thinking of proceedings which would be the only proper ones to pursue in time of peace, thought more of the utterly lawless condition of society surrounding him at the time of his dispatch and of what would prove a sure remedy. He never proposed to do an illegal act nor expressed determination to proceed beyond what the law in the future might authorize for the punishment of the atrocities which have been committed, and the commission of which can not be successfully denied. It is a deplorable fact that political crimes and murders have been committed in Louisiana which have gone unpunished, and which have been justified or apologized for, which must rest as a reproach upon the State and country long after the present generation had passed away.

I have no desire to have United States troops interfere in the domestic concerns of Louisiana or any other State.

On the 9th of December last Governor Kellogg telegraphed to me his apprehensions that the White League intended to make another attack upon the statehouse, to which, on the same day, I made the following answer, since which no communication has been sent to him:

> Your dispatch of this date just received. It is exceedingly unpalatable to use troops in anticipation of danger. Let the State authorities be right, and then proceed with their duties without apprehension of danger. If they are molested, the question will be deter-

mined whether the United States is able to maintain law and order within its limits or not.

I have deplored the necessity which seemed to make it my duty under the Constitution and laws to direct such interference. I have always refused except where it seemed to be my imperative duty to act in such a manner under the Constitution and laws of the United States. I have repeatedly and earnestly entreated the people of the South to live together in peace and obey the laws; and nothing would give me greater pleasure than to see reconciliation and tranquillity everywhere prevail, and thereby remove all necessity for the presence of troops among them. I regret, however, to say that this state of things does not exist, nor does its existence seem to be desired, in some localities; and as to those it may be proper for me to say that to the extent that Congress has conferred power upon me to prevent it neither Kuklux Klans, White Leagues, nor any other association using arms and violence to execute their unlawful purposes can be permitted in that way to govern any part of this country; nor can I see with indifference Union men or Republicans ostracized, persecuted, and murdered on account of their opinions, as they now are in some localities.

I have heretofore urged the case of Louisiana upon the attention of Congress, and I can not but think that its inaction has produced great evil.

To summarize: In September last an armed, organized body of men, in the support of candidates who had been put in nomination for the offices of governor and lieutenant-governor at the November election in 1872, and who had been declared not elected by the board of canvassers, recognized by all the courts to which the question had been submitted, undertook to subvert and overthrow the State Government that had been recognized by me in accordance with previous precedents. The recognized governor was driven from the statehouse, and but for his finding shelter in the United States custom-house, in the capital of the State of which he was governor, it is scarcely to be doubted that he would have been killed.

From the statehouse, before he had been driven to the custom-house, a call was made, in accordance with the fourth section, fourth article, of the Constitution of the United States, for the aid of the General Government to suppress domestic violence. Under those circumstances, and in accordance with my sworn duties, my proclamation of the 15th of September, 1874, was issued. This served to reinstate Governor Kellogg to his position nominally, but it can not be claimed that the insurgents have to this day surrendered to the State authorities the arms belonging to the State, or that they have in any sense disarmed. On the contrary, it is known that the same armed organizations that existed on the 14th of September, 1874, in opposition to the recognized State government, still retain their organization, equipments, and commanders, and can be called out at any hour to resist the State government. Under these circumstances the same military force has been continued in Louisiana as was sent there under the first call, and under the same general instructions. I repeat that the task assumed by the troops is not a pleasant one to them; that the Army is not composed of lawyers, capable of judging at a moment's notice of just how far they can go in the maintenance of law and order, and that it was impossible to give specific instructions providing for all possible contingencies that might arise. The troops were bound to act upon the judgment of the commanding officer upon each sudden contingency that arose, or wait instructions which could only reach them after the threatened wrongs had been committed which they were called on to prevent. It should be recollected, too, that upon my recognition of the Kellogg government I reported the fact, with the grounds of recognition, to Congress, and asked that body to take action in the matter; otherwise I should regard their silence as an acquiescence in my course. No action has been taken by that body, and I have maintained the position then marked out.

If error has been committed by the Army in these matters, it has always been on the side of the preservation of good order, the maintenance of law, and the protection of life. Their bearing reflects credit upon the soldiers, and if wrong has resulted the blame is with the turbulent element surrounding them.

I now earnestly ask that such action be taken by Congress as to leave my duties perfectly clear in dealing with the affairs of Louisiana, giving assurance at the same time that whatever may be done by that body in the premises will be executed according to the spirit and letter of the law, without fear or favor.

I herewith transmit copies of documents containing more specific information as to the subject-matter of the resolution.

U. S. GRANT

SEVENTH ANNUAL MESSAGE
December 7, 1875

*One of five vital points Grant wanted Congress to
tackle in 1875 still occupies the nation's attention:
"Declare church and state forever separate and distinct. . . ."*

To the Senate and House of Representatives:

In submitting my seventh annual message to Congress, in this centennial year of our national existence as a free and independent people, it
affords me great pleasure to recur to the advancement that has been made
from the time of the colonies, one hundred years ago. We were then a
people numbering only 3,000,000. Now we number more than 40,000,000.
Then industries were confined almost exclusively to the tillage of the soil.
Now manufactories absorb much of the labor of the country.

Our liberties remain unimpaired; the bondmen have been freed from
slavery; we have become possessed of the respect, if not the friendship,
of all civilized nations. . . .

We are a republic whereof one man is as good as another before the
law. Under such a form of government is is of the greatest importance
that all should be possessed of education and intelligence enough to cast
a vote with a right understanding of its meaning. . . . As the primary
step, therefore, to our advancement in all that has marked our progress
in the past century, I suggest for your earnest consideration, and most
earnestly recommend it, that a constitutional amendment be submitted to
the legislatures of the several States for ratification, making it the duty
of each of the several States to establish and forever maintain free public
schools adequate to the education of all the children in the rudimentary
branches within their respective limits, irrespective of sex, color, birth-
place, or religions; forbidding the teaching in said schools of religious,
atheistic, or pagan tenets; and prohibiting the granting of any school
funds or school taxes, or any part thereof, either by legislative, municipal,
or other authority, for the benefit or in aid, directly or indirectly, of any
religious sect or denomination, or in aid or for the benefit of any other
object of any nature or kind whatever.

In connection with this important question I would also call your attention to the importance of correcting an evil that, if permitted to continue,
will probably lead to great trouble in our land before the close of the
nineteenth century. It is the accumulation of vast amounts of untaxed
church property. . . .

I would suggest the taxation of all property equally, whether church
or corporation, exempting only the last resting place of the dead and
possibly, with proper restrictions, church edifices.

Our relations with most of the foreign powers continue on a satisfactory and friendly footing. . . .

In March last an arrangement was made, through Mr. Cushing, our minister in Madrid, with the Spanish Government for the payment by the latter to the United States of the sum of $80,000 in coin, for the purpose of the relief of the families or persons of the ship's company and certain passengers of the *Virginius*. . . .

The past year has furnished no evidence of an approaching termination of the ruinous conflict which has been raging for seven years in the neighboring island of Cuba. The same disregard of the laws of civilized warfare and of the just demands of humanity which has heretofore called forth expressions of condemnation from the nations of Christendom has continued to blacken the sad scene. Desolation, ruin, and pillage are pervading the rich fields of one of the most fertile and productive regions of the earth, and the incendiary's torch, firing plantations and valuable factories and buildings, is the agent marking the alternate advance or retreat of contending parties.

The protracted continuance of this strife seriously affects the interests of all commercial nations, but those of the United States more than others, by reason of close proximity, its larger trade and intercourse with Cuba, and the frequent and intimate personal and social relations which have grown up between its citizens and those of the island. Moreover, the property of our citizens in Cuba is large, and is rendered insecure and depreciated in value and in capacity of production by the continuance of the strife and the unnatural mode of its conduct. The same is true, differing only in degree, with respect to the interests and people of other nations; and the absence of any reasonable assurance of a near termination of the conflict must of necessity soon compel the States thus suffering to consider what the interests of their own people and their duty toward themselves may demand. . . .

A recognition of the independence of Cuba being, in my opinion, impracticable and indefensible, the question which next presents itself is that of the belligerent rights in the parties to the contest. . . .

Considered as a question of expediency, I regard the accordance of belligerent rights still to be as unwise and premature as I regard it to be, at present, indefensible as a measure of right. . . .

. . . I hope Congress may be induced, at the earliest day practicable, to insure the consummation of the act of the last Congress, at its last session, to bring about specie resumption "on and after the 1st of January, 1879," at furthest. . . .

The discovery of gold in the Black Hills, a portion of the Sioux Reservation, has had the effect to induce a large emigration of miners to that point. Thus far the effort to protect the treaty rights of the Indians to that section has been successful, but the next year will certainly witness a large increase of such emigration. . . .

As this will be the last annual message which I shall have the honor of transmitting to Congress before my successor is chosen, I will repeat or recapitulate the questions which I deem of vital importance which may be legislated upon and settled at this session:

First. That the States shall be required to afford the opportunity of a good common-school education to every child within their limits.

Second. No sectarian tenets shall ever be taught in any school supported in whole or in part by the State, nation, or by the proceeds of any tax levied upon any community. Make education compulsory so far as to deprive all persons who can not read and white from becoming voters after the year 1890, disfranchising none, however, on grounds of illiteracy who may be voters at the time this amendment takes effect.

Third. Declare church and state forever separate and distinct, but each free within their proper spheres; and that all church property shall bear its own proportion of taxation.

Fourth. Drive out licensed immorality, such as polygamy and the importation of women for illegitimate purposes. To recur again to the centennial year, it would seem as though now, as we are about to begin the second century of our national existence, would be a most fitting time for these reforms.

Fifth. Enact such laws as will insure a speedy return to a sound currency, such as will command the respect of the world.

Believing that these views will commend themselves to the great majority of the right-thinking and patriotic citizens of the United States, I submit the rest to Congress.

ON EXECUTIVE ACTS
May 4, 1876

When the House demanded information that Grant
felt was an infringement on the rights of the Executive
branch of the Government, he replied bluntly.

To the House of Representatives:

I have given very attentive consideration to a resolution of the House
of Representatives passed on the 3d of April, requesting the President of
the United States to inform the House whether any executive offices, acts,
or duties, and, if any, what, have within a specified period been performed at a distance from the seat of Government established by law, etc.

I have never hesitated and shall not hesitate to communicate to Congress, and to either branch thereof, all the information which the Constitution makes it the duty of the President to give, or which my judgment
may suggest to me or a request from either House may indicate to me
will be useful in the discharge of the appropriate duties confided to them.
I fail, however, to find in the Constitution of the United States the authority given to the House of Representatives (one branch of the Congress, in which is vested the legislative power of the Government) to require of the Executive, an independent branch of the Government, coordinate with the Senate and House of Representatives, an account of his
discharge of his appropriate and purely executive offices, acts, and duties,
either as to when, where, or how performed.

What the House of Representatives may require as a right in its demand upon the Executive for information is limited to what is necessary
for the proper discharge of its powers of legislation or of impeachment.

The inquiry in the resolution of the House as to where executive acts
have within the last seven years been performed and at what distance
from any particular spot or for how long a period at any one time, etc.,
does not necessarily belong to the province of legislation. It does not
profess to be asked for that object.

If this information be sought through an inquiry of the President as to
his executive acts in view or in aid of the power of impeachment vested
in the House, it is asked in derogation of an inherent natural right,
recognized in this country by a constitutional guaranty which protects
every citizen, the President as well as the humblest in the land, from
being made a witness against himself.

During the time that I have had the honor to occupy the position of
President of this Government it has been, and while I continue to occupy
that position it will continue to be, my earnest endeavor to recognize and
to respect the several trusts and duties and powers of the coordinate
branches of the Government, not encroaching upon them nor allowing
encroachments upon the proper powers of the office which the people of

the United States have confided to me, but aiming to preserve in their proper relations the several powers and functions of each of the coordinate branches of the Government, agreeably to the Constitution and in accordance with the solemn oath which I have taken to "preserve, protect, and defend" that instrument.

In maintenance of the rights secured by the Constitution to the executive branch of the Government I am compelled to decline any specific or detailed answer to the request of the House for information as to "any executive offices, acts, or duties, and if any, what, have been performed at a distance from the seat of Government established by law, and for how long a period at any one time and in what part of the United States."

If, however, the House of Representatives desires to know whether during the period of upward of seven years during which I have held the office of President of the United States I have been absent from the seat of Government, and whether during that period I have performed or have neglected to perform the duties of my office, I freely inform the House that from the time of my entrance upon my office I have been in the habit, as were all of my predecessors (with the exception of one, who lived only one month after assuming the duties of his office, and one whose continued presence in Washington was necessary from the existence at the time of a powerful rebellion), of absenting myself at times from the seat of Government, and that during such absences I did not neglect or forego the obligations or the duties of my office, but continued to discharge all of the executive offices, acts, and duties which were required of me as the President of the United States. I am not aware that a failure occurred in any one instance of my exercising the functions and powers of my office in every case requiring their discharge, or of my exercising all necessary executive acts, in whatever part of the United States I may at the time have been. Fortunately, the rapidity of travel and of mail communications and the facility of almost instantaneous correspondence with the offices at the seat of Government, which the telegraph affords to the President in whatever section of the Union he may be, enable him in these days to maintain as constant and almost as quick intercourse with the Departments at Washington as may be maintained while he remains at the capital.

The necessity of the performance of executive acts by the President of the United States exists and is devolved upon him, wherever he may be within the United States, during his term of office by the Constitution of the United States.

His civil powers are no more limited or capable of limitation as to the place where they shall be exercised than are those which he might be required to discharge in his capacity of Commander in Chief of the Army and Navy, which latter powers it is evident he might be called upon to exercise, possibly, even without the limits of the United States. Had the efforts of those recently in rebellion against the Government been successful in driving a late President of the United States from Washington, it is manifest that he must have discharged his functions, both civil and military, elsewhere than in the place named by law as the seat of Government.

No act of Congress can limit, suspend, or confine this constitutional duty. I am not aware of the existence of any act of Congress which assumes thus to limit or restrict the exercise of the functions of the Executive. Were there such acts, I should nevertheless recognize the superior authority of the Constitution, and should exercise the powers required thereby of the President.

The act to which reference is made in the resolution of the House relates to the establishing of the seat of Government and the providing of suitable buildings and removal thereto of the offices attached to the Government, etc. It was not understood at its date and by General Washington to confine the President in the discharge of his duties and powers to actual presence at the seat of Government. On the 30th of March, 1791, shortly after the passage of the act referred to, General Washington issued an Executive proclamation having reference to the subject of this very act from Georgetown, a place remote from Philadelphia, which then was the seat of Government, where the act referred to directed that "all the offices attached to the seat of Government" should for the time remain.

That none of his successors have entertained the idea that their executive offices could be performed only at the seat of Government is evidenced by the hundreds upon hundreds of such acts performed by my predecessors in unbroken line from Washington to Lincoln, a memorandum of the general nature and character of some of which acts is submitted herewith; and no question has ever been raised as to the validity of those acts or as to the right and propriety of the Executive to exercise the powers of his office in any part of the United States.

EIGHTH ANNUAL MESSAGE
December 5, 1876

In an astonishing message of apology as his eight years of office were drawing to a close, Grant laid blame for failures on "errors of judgment, not of intent." He concluded with a justification of a policy dear to him: annexation of Santo Domingo.

To the Senate and House of Representatives:

In submitting my eighth and last annual message to Congress it seems proper that I should refer to and in some degree recapitulate the events and official acts of the past eight years.

It was my fortune, or misfortune, to be called to the office of Chief Executive without any previous political training. From the age of 17 I had never even witnessed the excitement attending a Presidential campaign but twice antecedent to my own candidacy, and at but one of them was I eligible as a voter.

Under such circumstances it is but reasonable to suppose that errors of judgment must have occurred. Even had they not, differences of opinion between the Executive, bound by an oath to the strict performance of his duties, and writers and debaters must have arisen. It is not necessarily evidence of blunder on the part of the Executive because there are these differences of views. Mistakes have been made, as all can see and I admit, but it seems to me oftener in the selections made of the assistants appointed to aid in carrying out the various duties of administering the Government—in nearly ever case selected without a personal acquaintance with the appointee, but upon recommendations of the representatives chosen directly by the people. It is impossible, where so many trusts are to be allotted, that the right parties should be chosen in every instance. History shows that no Administration from the time of Washington the the present has been free from these mistakes. But I leave comparisons to history, claiming only that I have acted in every instance from a conscientious desire to do what was right, constitutional, within the law, and for the very best interests of the whole people. Failures have been errors of judgment, not of intent.

My civil career commenced, too, at a most critical and difficult time. Less than four years before, the country had emerged from a conflict such as no other nation had ever survived. Nearly one-half of the States had revolted against the Government, and of those remaining faithful to the Union a large percentage of the population sympathized with the rebellion and made an "enemy in the rear" almost as dangerous as the more honorable enemy in the front. The latter committed errors of judgment, but they maintained them openly and courageously; the former received the protection of the Government they would see destroyed, and reaped all the pecuniary advantage to be gained out of the then existing state of affairs, many of them by obtaining contracts and by swindling the Government in the delivery of their goods.

Immediately on the cessation of hostilities the then noble President, who had carried the country so far through its perils, fell a martyr to his patriotism at the hands of an assassin.

The intervening time to my first inauguration was filled up with wranglings between Congress and the new Executive as to the best mode of "reconstruction," or, to speak plainly, as to whether the control of the Government should be thrown immediately into the hands of those who had so recently and persistently tried to destroy it, or whether the victors should continue to have an equal voice with them in this control. Reconstruction, as finally agreed upon, means this and only this, except that the late slave was enfranchised, giving an increase, as was supposed, to the Union-loving and Union-supporting votes. If *free* in the full sense of the word, they would not disappoint this expectation. Hence at the beginning of my first Administration the work of reconstruction, much embarrassed by the long delay, virtually commenced. It was the work of the legislative branch of the Government. My province was wholly in approving their acts, which I did most heartily, urging the legislatures of States that had not yet done so to ratify the fifteenth amendment to the Constitution. The country was laboring under an enormous debt, contracted in the suppression of rebellion, and taxation was so oppressive as to discourage production. Another danger also threatened us—a foreign war. The last difficulty had to be adjusted and was adjusted without a war and in a manner highly honorable to all parties concerned. Taxes have been reduced within the last seven years nearly $300,000,000, and the national debt has been reduced in the same time over $435,000,000. By refunding the 6 per cent bonded debt for bonds bearing 5 and 4-1/2 per cent interest, respectively, the annual interest has been reduced from over $130,000,000 in 1869 to but little over $100,000,000 in 1876. The balance of trade has been changed from over $130,000,000 against the United States in 1869 to more than $120,000,000 in our favor in 1876.

It is confidently believed that the balance of trade in favor of the United States will increase, not diminish, and that the pledge of Congress to resume specie payments in 1879 will be easily accomplished, even in the absence of much-desired further legislation on the subject.

A policy has been adopted toward the Indian tribes inhabiting a large portion of the territory of the United States which has been humane and has substantially ended Indian hostilities in the whole land except in a portion of Nebraska, and Dakota, Wyoming, and Montana Territories—the Black Hills region and approaches thereto. Hostilities there have grown out of the avarice of the white man, who has violated our treaty stipulations in his search for gold. The question might be asked why the Government has not enforced obedience to the terms of the treaty prohibiting the occupation of the Black Hills region by whites. The answer is simple: The first immigrants to the Black Hills were removed by troops, but rumors of rich discoveries of gold took into that region increased numbers. Gold has actually been found in paying quantity, and an effort to remove the miners would only result in the desertion of the bulk of the troops that might be sent there to remove them. All difficulty in this matter has, however, been removed—subject to the approval of Congress—by a treaty ceding the Black Hills and approaches to settlement by citizens. . . .

The cordiality which attends our relations with the powers of the earth has been plainly shown by the general participation of foreign nations in the exhibition which has just closed and by the exertions made by distant powers to show their interest in and friendly feelings toward the United States in the commemoration of the centennial of the nation. . . .

The Court of Commissioners of Alabama Claims, whose functions were continued by an act of the last session of Congress until the 1st day of January, 1877, has carried on its labors with diligence and general satisfaction. By a report from the clerk of the court, transmitted herewith, bearing date November 14, 1876, it appears that within the time now allowed by law the court will have disposed of all the claims presented for adjudication. . . .

It is with satisfaction that I am enabled to state that the work of the joint commission for determining the boundary line between the United States and British possessions from the northwest angle of the Lake of the Woods to the Rocky Mountains, commenced in 1872, has been completed. The final agreements of the commissioners, with the maps, have been duly signed, and the work of the commission is complete.

The fixing of the boundary upon the Pacific coast by the protocol of March 10, 1873, pursuant to the award of the Emperor of Germany by Article XXXIV of the treaty of Washington, with the termination of the work of this commission, adjusts and fixes the entire boundary between the United States and the British possessions, except as to the portion of territory ceded by Russia to the United States under the treaty of 1867. The work intrusted to the commissioner and the officers of the Army attached to the commission has been well and satisfactorily performed. . . .

The necessary legislation to carry into effect the convention respecting commercial reciprocity concluded with the Hawaiian Islands in 1875 having been had, the proclamation to carry into effect the convention, as provided by the act approved August 15, 1876, was duly issued upon the 9th day of September last. . . .

The commotions which have been prevalent in Mexico for some time past, and which, unhappily, seem to be not yet wholly quieted, have led to complaints of citizens of the United States of injuries by persons in authority. It is hoped, however, that these will ultimately be adjusted to the satisfaction of both Governments. . . .

It is with satisfaction that I am able to announce that the joint commission for the adjustment of claims between the United States and Mexico under the convention of 1868, the duration of which has been several times extended, has brought its labors to a close.

The report of the Secretary of the Navy shows that branch of the service to be in condition as effective as it is possible to keep it with the means and authority given the Department. It is, of course, not possible to rival the costly and progressive establishments of great European powers with the old material of our Navy, to which no increase has been authorized since the war, except the eight small cruisers built to supply the place of others which had gone to decay. Yet the most has been done that was possible with the means at command; and by substantially rebuilding some of our old ships with durable material and completely repairing and refitting our monitor fleet the Navy has been gradually so brought up that, though it does not maintain its relative position among the progressive navies of the world, it is now in a condition more powerful and effective than it ever has been in time of peace. . . .

A few postmasters in the Southern States have expressed great apprehension of their personal safety on account of their connection with the postal service, and have specially requested that their reports of apprehended danger should not be made public lest it should result in the loss of their lives. But no positive testimony of interference has been submitted, except in the case of a mail messenger at Spartanburg, in South Carolina, who reported that he had been violently driven away while in charge of the mails on account of his political affiliations. An assistant superintendent of the Railway Mail Service investigated this case and reported that the messenger had disappeared from his post, leaving his work to be performed by a substitute. The Postmaster-General thinks this case is sufficiently suggestive to justify him in recommending that a more severe punishment should be provided for the offense of assaulting any person in charge of the mails or of retarding or otherwise obstructing them by threats of personal injury. . . .

The international exhibition held in Philadelphia this year, in commemoration of the one hundredth anniversary of American independence, has proven a great success, and will, no doubt, be of enduring advantage to the country. . . .

The attention of Congress can not be too earnestly called to the necessity of throwing some greater safeguard over the method of choosing and declaring the election of a President. Under the present system there seems to be no provided remedy for contesting the election in any one State. The remedy is partially, no doubt, in the enlightenment of electors. The compulsory support of the free school and the disfranchisement of all who can not read and write the English language, after a fixed probation, would meet my hearty approval. I would not make this apply, however, to those already voters, but I would to all becoming so after the expiration of the probation fixed upon. Foreigners coming to this country to become citizens, who are educated in their own language, should acquire the requisite knowledge of ours during the necessary residence to obtain naturalization. If they did not take interest enough in our language to acquire sufficient knowledge of it to enable them to study the institutions and laws of the country intelligently, I would not confer upon them the right to make such laws nor to select those who do.

I append to this message, for convenient reference, a synopsis of administrative events and of all recommendations to Congress made by me during the last seven years. Time may show some of these recommendations not to have been wisely conceived, but I believe the larger part will do no discredit to the Administration. One of these recommendations met with the united opposition of one political party in the Senate and with a strong opposition from the other, namely, the treaty for the annexation of Santo Domingo to the United States, to which I will specially refer, maintaining, as I do, that if my views had been concurred in the country would be in a more prosperous condition to-day, both politically and financially.

Santo Domingo is fertile, and upon its soil may be grown just those tropical products of which the United States use so much, and which are produced or prepared for market now by slave labor almost exclusively, namely, sugar, coffee, dye woods, mahogany, tropical fruits, tobacco, etc. About 75 per cent of the exports of Cuba are consumed in the United States. A large percentage of the exports of Brazil also find the same market. These are paid for almost exclusively in coin, legislation, particularly in Cuba, being unfavorable to a mutual exchange of the products of each country. Flour shipped from the Mississippi River to Havana can pass by the very entrance to the city on its way to a port in Spain, there pay a duty fixed upon articles to be reexported, transferred to a Spanish vessel and brought back almost to the point of starting, paying a second duty, and still leave a profit over what would be received by direct shipment. All that is produced in Cuba could be produced in Santo Domingo. Being a part of the United States, commerce between the island and mainland would be free. There would be no export duties on her shipments nor import duties on those coming here. There would be no import duties upon the supplies, machinery, etc., going from the States. The effect that would have been produced upon Cuba commerce, with these advantages to a rival, is observable at a glance. The Cuban question would have been settled long ago in favor of "free Cuba." Hundreds of American vessels would now be advantageously used in transporting the valuable woods and other products of the soil of the island to a market and in carrying supplies and emigrants to it. The island is but sparsely settled, while it has an area sufficient for the profitable employment of several millions of people. The soil would have soon fallen into the hands of United States capitalists. The products are so valuable in commerce that emigration there would have been encouraged; the emancipated race of the South would have found there a congenial home where their civil rights would not be disputed and where their labor would be so much sought after that the poorest among them could have found the means to go. Thus in cases of great oppression and cruelty such has been practiced upon them in many places within the last eleven years, whole communities would have sought refuge in Santo Domingo. I do not suppose the whole race would have gone, nor is it desirable that they should go. Their labor is desirable—indispensable almost where they now are. But the possession of this territory would have left the negro "master of the situation," by enabling him to demand his rights at home on pain of finding them elsewhere.

I do not present these views now as a recommendation for a renewal of the subject of annexation, but I do refer to it to vindicate my previous action in regard to it.

With the present term of Congress my official life terminates. It is not probable that public affairs will ever again receive attention from me further than as a citizen of the Republic, always taking a deep interest in the honor, integrity, and prosperity of the whole land.

ON USE OF TROOPS IN THE SOUTH
January 22, 1877

President Grant defended the constitutional use of
Federal troops to keep order in the states.

To the House of Representatives:

On the 9th day of December, 1876, the following resolution of the House of Representatives was received, namely:

Resolved, That the President be requested, if not incompatible with the public interest, to transmit to this House copies of any and all orders or directions emanating from him or from either of the Executive Departments of the Government to any military commander or civil officer with reference to the service of the Army, or any portion thereof, in the States of Virginia, South Carolina, Louisiana, and Florida since the 1st of August last, together with reports by telegraph or otherwise from either or any of said military commanders or civil officers.

It was immediately or soon thereafter referred to the Secretary of War and the Attorney-General, the custodians of all retained copies of "orders or directions" given by the Executive Departments of the Government covered by the above inquiry, together with all information upon which such "orders or directions" were given.

The information, it will be observed, is voluminous, and, with the limited clerical force in the Department of Justice, has consumed the time up to the present. Many of the communications accompanying this have been already made public in connection with messages heretofore sent to Congress. This class of information includes the important documents received from the governor of South Carolina and sent to Congress with my message on the subject of the Hamburg massacre; also the documents accompanying my response to the resolution of the House of Representatives in regard to the soldiers stationed at Petersburg.

There have also come to me and to the Department of Justice, from time to time, other earnest written communications from persons holding public trusts and from others residing in the South, some of which I append hereto as bearing upon the precarious condition of the public peace in those States. These communications I have reason to regard as made by respectable and responsible men. Many of them deprecate the publication of their names as involving danger to them personally.

The reports heretofore made by committees of Congress of the results of their inquiries in Mississippi and Louisiana, and the newspapers of several States recommending "the Mississippi plan," have also furnished important data for estimating the danger to the public peace and order in those States.

It is enough to say that these different kinds and sources of evidence have left no doubt whatever in my mind that intimidation has been used, and actual violence, to an extent requiring the aid of the United States Government, where it was practicable to furnish such aid, in South Carolina, in Florida, and in Louisiana, as well as in Mississippi, in Alabama, and in Georgia.

The troops of the United States have been but sparingly used, and in no case so as to interfere with the free exercise of the right of suffrage. Very few troops were available for the purpose of preventing or suppressing the violence and intimidation existing in the States above named. In no case, except that of South Carolina, was the number of soldiers in any State increased in anticipation of the election, saving that twenty-four men and an officer were sent from Fort Foote to Petersburg, Va., where disturbances were threatened prior to the election.

No troops were stationed at the voting places. In Florida and in Louisiana, respectively, the small number of soldiers already in the said States were stationed at such points in each State as were most threatened with violence, where they might be available as a posse for the officer whose duty it was to preserve the peace and prevent intimidation of voters. Such a disposition of the troops seemed to me reasonable and justified by law and precedent, while its omission would have been inconsistent with the constitutional duty of the President of the United States "to take care that the laws be faithfully executed." The statute expressly forbids the bringing of troops to the polls "except where it is necessary to keep the peace,'' implying that to keep the peace it may be done. But this even, so far as I am advised, has not in any case been done. The stationing of a company or part of a company in the vicinity, where they would be available to prevent riot, has been the only use made of troops prior to and at the time of the elections. Where so stationed, they could be called in an emergency requiring it by a marshal or deputy marshal as a posse to aid in suppressing unlawful violence. The evidence which has come to me has left me no ground to doubt that if there had been more military force available it would have been my duty to have disposed of it in several States with a view to the prevention of the violence and intimidation which have undoubtedly contributed to the defeat of the election law in Mississippi, Alabama, and Georgia, as well as in South Carolina, Louisiana, and Florida.

By Article IV, section 4, of the Constitution—

The United States shall guarantee to every State in this Union a republican form of government, and shall protect each of them against invasion, and on application of the legislature, or of the executive (when the legislature can not be convened), against domestic violence.

By act of Congress (U.S. Revised Statutes, secs. 1034, 1035) the President, in case of "insurrection in any State" or of "unlawful obstruction to the enforcement of the laws of the United States by the ordinary course of judicial proceedings," or whenever "domestic violence in any State so obstructs the execution of the laws thereof and of the United States as to deprive any portion of the people of such State" of their civil or political rights, is authorized to employ such parts of the land and naval forces as he may deem necessary to enforce the execution of the laws and preserve the peace and sustain the authority of the State and of the United States. Acting under this title (69) of the Revised Statutes United States, I accompanied the sending of troops to South Carolina with a proclamation such as is therein prescribed.

The President is also authorized by act of Congress "to employ such part of the land or naval forces of the United States * * * as shall be necessary to prevent the violation and to enforce the due execution of the provisions" of title 24 of the Revised Statutes of the United States, for the protection of the civil rights of citizens, among which is the provision against conspiracies "to prevent, by force, intimidation, or threat, any citizen who is lawfully entitled to vote from giving his support or advocacy in a legal manner toward or in favor of the election of any lawfully qualified person as an elector for President or Vice-President or as a member of Congress of the United States." (U. S. Revised Statutes, sec. 1989.)

In cases falling under this title I have not considered it necessary to issue a proclamation to precede or accompany the employment of such part of the Army as seemed to be necessary.

In case of insurrection against a State government or against the Government of the United States a proclamation is appropriate; but in keeping the peace of the United States at an election at which Members of Congress are elected no such call from the State or proclamation by the President is prescribed by statute or required by precedent.

In the case of South Carolina insurrection and domestic violence against the State government were clearly shown, and the application of the governor founded thereon was duly presented, and I could not deny his constitutional request without abandoning my duty as the Executive of the National Government.

The companies stationed in the other States have been employed to secure the better execution of the laws of the United States and to preserve the peace of the United States.

After the election had been had, and where violence was apprehended by which the returns from the counties and precincts might be destroyed, troops were ordered to the State of Florida, and those already in Louisiana were ordered to the points in greatest danger of violence.

I have not employed troops on slight occasions, nor in any case where it has not been necessary to the enforcement of the laws of the United States. In this I have been guided by the Constitution and the laws which have been enacted and the precedents which have been formed under it.

It has been necessary to employ troops occasionally to overcome resistance to the internal-revenue laws from the time of the resistance to the collection of the whisky tax in Pennsylvania, under Washington, to the present time.

In 1854, when it was apprehended that resistance would be made in Boston to the seizure and return to his master of a fugitive slave, the troops there stationed were employed to enforce the master's right under the Constitution, and troops stationed at New York were ordered to be in readiness to go to Boston if it should prove to be necessary.

In 1859, when John Brown, with a small number of men, made his attack upon Harpers Ferry, the President ordered United States troops to assist in the apprehension and suppression of him and his party without a formal call of the legislature or governor of Virginia and without proclamation of the President.

Without citing further instances in which the Executive has exercised his power, as Commander of the Army and Navy, to prevent or suppress resistance to the laws of the United States, or where he has exercised like authority in obedience to a call from a State to suppress insurrection, I desire to assure both Congress and the country that it has been my purpose to administer the executive powers of the Government fairly, and in no instance to disregard or transcend the limits of the Constitution.

U. S. GRANT

BIBLIOGRAPHICAL AIDS

BIBLIOGRAPHICAL AIDS

The emphasis in this and subsequent volumes of the Presidential Chronologies series will be on the administrations of the presidents. The more important works on other aspects of their lives, either before or after their terms, are included since they may contribute to an understanding of the presidential careers.

The following bibliography is critically selected. Many additional titles may be found in the Hesseltine bibliography (see Biographies below) and in the standard guide. The student might also wish to consult **Reader's Guide to Periodical Literature** and **Social Sciences and Humanities Index** (formerly **International Index**) for recent articles in scholarly journals.

Additional chronological information not included in this volume because it did not relate directly to the president may be found in the **Encyclopedia of American History,** edited by Richard B. Morris, revised edition (New York, 1965).

Asterisks after titles refer to books currently available in paperback editions.

SOURCE MATERIALS

Compared with some of the presidents Ulysses S. Grant left no voluminous stock of personal papers to posterity. The Library of Congress contains some papers, mainly wartime records, and other collections of his papers and letters can be found at the Illinois State Historical Library in Springfield, the Princeton University Library and the Rutherford B. Hayes Library in Fremont, Ohio. Other pieces are in Chicago Historical Society and New York Historical Society collections.

The papers in The Library of Congress are available on microfilm and an index has been prepared for them. In addition, Southern Illinois University has begun the publication of Grant's papers, with Volume I, covering the years to the Civil War, appearing in 1967.

Grant, Ulysses S. **Index to Ulysses S. Grant's Papers.** Washington, D.C., 1965.* 83 p. 70¢ Catalog No. LC 4.7: G76.

Presidential Papers Microfilm: Ulysses S. Grant Papers. Washington, D.C., 1965.

Simon, John Y. **The Papers of Ulysses S. Grant.** Volume I, 1837-1861. Carbondale, Illinois, 1967.

BIOGRAPHIES

Catton, Bruce. **U.S. Grant and the American Military Tradition.** Boston, 1954.* Although only 27 pages are devoted to Grant's years in the presidency, this treatment by the Civil War historian points up the temper of the times, observing that Grant's failures were more of omission rather than commission.

Church, William Conant. **Ulysses S. Grant and the Period of National Preservation and Reconstruction.** New York, 1926. Includes much detail of Grant's life.

Grant, Ulysses S. **Personal Memoirs.** 2 vols. New York, 1885. Also in new ed. by E.B. Long, 1 vol. Cleveland, 1952. Thoroughly readable, this autobiography concludes with the end of the Civil War.

Hesseltine, William B. **Ulysses S. Grant, Politician.** New York, 1957. This standard biography of Grant gives a good view of his years in the presidency.

Lewis, Lloyd. **Captain Sam Grant.** Boston, 1950. A perceptive study of Grant's life up to the Civil War.

Nevins, Allan. **Hamilton Fish: The Inner History of the Grant Administration.** New York, 1936. Essential to an understanding of the Grant administration. Based on Fish's copious records for the eight year period in which he was Secretary of State.

Woodward, William E. **Meet General Grant.** rev. ed. New York, 1946. This popularized biography debunks many of the criticisms of Grant.

MILITARY STUDIES

Badeau, Adam. **Military History of Ulysses S. Grant from April 1861 to April 1865.** 3 vol. New York, 1868-81. A contemporary view, though biased.

Cadwallader, Sylvanus. **Three Years with Grant.** ed. by Banjamin P. Thomas. New York, 1955. The colorful and intimate recollections of a war correspondent.

Catton, Bruce. **Grant Moves South.** Boston, 1960. Developed from the notes of the late Lloyd Lewis, this book picks up where **Captain Sam Grant** left off in 1861 and continues through the Vicksburg campaign. Also recommended are Catton's other works on the Civil War, including **A Stillness at Appomattox,** New York, 1963, and **This Hallowed Ground,** New York, 1956.

Freeman, Douglas S. **Lee's Lieutenants.** 3 vol. New York, 1942-44. A comprehensive view of the Confederate military leadership.

Fuller, John F. C. **The Generalship of Ulysses S. Grant.** New York, 1929.

Fuller, J.F.C. **Grant and Lee: A Study in Personality and Generalship.** Bloomington, 1957. An appraisal of the merits of the two opponents by a Briton, with Grant taking the honors.

Miers, Earl Schenck. **The Web of Victory: Grant at Vicksburg.** New York, 1955. A detailed account of the campaign.

Porter, Horace. **Campaigning with Grant.** ed. by W.C. Temple. Bloomington, 1961. The memoirs of Grant's aide-de-camp from April, 1864.

Randall, J.G., and Donald, David. **The Civil War and Reconstruction.** 2nd ed. Boston, 1961. This standard work contains an 86-page bibliography.

Williams, Kenneth P. **Lincoln Finds a General.** 5 vol. New York, 1949-59. Traverses the ups and downs of Union generalship through the war years.

ESSAYS

Most of the articles on Grant in encyclopedias concentrate on his Civil War years. However, the student would be well advised to direct his attention to the lengthy and scholarly article by David Donald in the **Encyclopedia Americana.** An extensive bibliography is included. For other aspects of Grant, consult the following:

Arnold, Matthew. **General Grant, with a Rejoinder by Mark Twain,** ed. by John Y. Simon. Carbondale, Illinois, 1966. The essay is mainly a sympathetic resume of Grant's **Personal Memoirs,** but a few mild comments sparked Twain's retort.

Hyman, H.M. "Johnson, Stanton, and Grant: A Reconsideration of the Army's Role in the Events Leading to Impeachment," **The American Historical Review** (October, 1960).

McPherson, J.M. "Grant or Greeley? The Abolitionist Dilemma in the Election of 1872," **The American Historical Review** (October, 1965).

THE RECONSTRUCTION ERA

Beale, Howard K. **The Critical Year; A Study of Andrew Johnson and Reconstruction.** New York, 1930 (1958).

Bowers, Claude G. **The Tragic Era; The Revolution After Lincoln.** Cambridge, 1929 (1962).*

Brock, William R. **An American Crisis: Congress and Reconstruction, 1865-1867.** New York, 1963.*

Buckmaster, Henrietta. **Freedom Bound.** New York, 1965.*

Carter, Hodding. **The Angry Scar; The Story of Reconstruction.** New York, 1959.

Cox, LaWanda C. and John H. **Politics, Principle, and Prejudice, 1865-1866; Dilemma of Reconstruction America.** New York, 1963.

Current, Richard N., ed. **Reconstruction, 1865-1877.** Englewood Cliffs, New Jersey, 1965.*

DuBois, William E.B. **Black Reconstruction in America, 1860-1880.** Cleveland, 1935 (1962).*

Dunning, William A. **Reconstruction, Political and Economic, 1865-1877.** New York, 1907 (1963).*

Fleming, Walter L., ed. **Documentary History of Reconstruction.** 2 vols., New York, 1966.*

Franklin, John H. **Reconstruction: After the Civil War.** Chicago, 1961.*

Hesseltine, William B., ed. **The Tragic Conflict; The Civil War and Reconstruction.** New York, 1962.

Lynd, Staughton, ed. **Reconstruction.** New York, 1967.*

McKitrick, Eric L. **Andrew Johnson and Reconstruction.** Chicago, 1960.*

Patrick, Rembert W. **The Reconstruction of the Nation.** New York, 1967.*

Randall, James G., and Donald, David. **The Civil War and Reconstruction.** Boston, 1961.

Rozwenc, Edwin C., ed. **Reconstruction in the South.** Boston, 1952.*

Shenton, James P. **The Reconstruction; A Documentary History of the South After the War.** New York, 1963.*

Stampp, Kenneth M. **The Era of Reconstruction, 1865-1877.** New York, 1965.*

Woodward, Comer V. **Reunion and Reaction; The Compromise of 1877 and the End of Reconstruction.** Revised and enlarged ed. New York, 1956.*

NAME INDEX

Seymour, Horatio, 6
Sherman, William T., 7
Stanton, Edwin M., 5, 8
Stewart, Alexander T., 6
Strong, William, 8, 9
Sumner, Charles, 8, 9

Taft, Alphonso, 14
Taylor, Zachary, 1
Tilden, Samuel J., 15
Twain, Mark, 17

Tyner, James N., 15

Vanderbilt, William H., 16

Waite, Morrison R., 12
Ward, Ferdinand, 16
Washburne, Elihu B., 6
Williams, George H., 10, 12, 13
Wilson, Henry, 10, 11, 14

Yates, Richard, 3